Remaking the World Bank

The critical problems of the developing countries threaten the health of the entire world economy, and the World Bank must play a larger role in responding to them.

To do so, the Bank must

- adapt its operations to recent changes in the international environment and help formulate and implement a viable strategy for resolving the lingering debt crisis both in the semi-industrialized and the poorest countries;

- take the lead in promoting greater coordination among all lenders, both private and official, to developing countries; especially it should broaden and deepen its collaboration with the International Monetary Fund and with private banks;

- reinforce the links between its lending and the adoption of sound policies by developing countries, including the strengthening of the private sector; and

- work for the expansion of its resources through an increase in its capital and through continued support by its member governments for the International Development Association, the Bank's arm for assistance to the poorest countries.

Remaking
the World Bank

Barend A. de Vries

Foreword by I.G. Patel

Seven Locks Press
Publishers
Washington, DC/Cabin John, MD

Copyright © 1987 by Barend A. de Vries

Library of Congress Cataloging-in-Publication Data

De Vries, Barend A.
  Remaking the World Bank

  Bibliography: p.
  Includes index.
  1. World Bank. I. Title.
HG3881.5.W57D4 1987   332.1'532   87-23406
ISBN 0-932020-49-6 (pbk.)

Manufactured in the United States of America

Design by Daniel Thomas

Seven Locks Press
Publishers
P.O. Box 27
Cabin John, Maryland 20818
(301) 320-2130

Books of Seven Locks Press are distributed to the trade by

National Book Network
4720 A Boston Way
Lanham, Maryland 20706

To Margaret

Contents

Foreword

VERY FEW PEOPLE remember now that the inspiration for the creation of the World Bank came essentially from the United States. The British, with their worries about their balance of payments after the war, were concerned only with the International Monetary Fund. It was in the hope of inducing the Russians also to join in postwar economic cooperation that U.S. officials thought of a bank for reconstruction; and the few developing countries present during the Bretton Woods negotiations naturally extended the idea to include "development."

Many things have happened since those halcyon days of postwar idealism to dampen our spirits. The Russians, for example, have not joined the Bretton Woods institutions. But it would, I think, be generally agreed that the World Bank has grown into a robust institution. It has moved with the times and taken new initiatives to meet new needs. When it became clear toward the end of the fifties that the urgent needs of many developing countries for capital could not be met on World Bank terms, despite those terms being somewhat more liberal than those for funds mobilized through private commercial channels, the Bank took the initiative in organizing aid consortia and created the International Development Association. The International

Finance Corporation was created to help the developing countries mobilize venture capital. Project lending came to be supplemented by program lending; and the preponderant support to economic infrastructure was replaced by increasing attention to building up human capital and meeting urgent social needs. Financing of local currency costs or public sector projects, once a taboo, became a not uncommon practice, at least for IDA.

From time to time, the Bank inevitably got caught up in acrimonious debates about appropriate policies or performance criteria. But it is fair to say that the Bank has endeavored to put the development dialogue on a fair and principled track by encouraging research and not losing sight of its basic objectives. Its American presidents, almost without exception, have been advocates of development first and have reflected their nationality only in that their advocacy has often had to be addressed largely to fellow Americans.

Why, then, are doubts about the future of the Bank expressed increasingly these days? Undoubtedly, there has been an ideological swing in the West generally in favor of more laissez-faire policies.

For the extremists of the New Right, there is no room for cooperation, let alone positive discrimination, in favor of the poor and the weak. At the same time, the advocates of "each for himself" are not averse to flexing their economic and political muscles for private or national gain. The debt crisis has eroded faith in the creditworthiness of developing countries and, dare one say, in the wisdom of private capital markets and of macroeconomic management generally. Objective conditions are also changing in a perverse way, with the most powerful country in the world becoming the greatest debtor, and there are signs of declining saving propensities in many of the richer countries. No one really knows what the rapid development of new technologies is doing to the comparative rates of return on capital in developing as against developed countries. At the same time, the political cauldron keeps boiling globally, as well as in many sensitive regions, consuming much-needed resources and creating new and complex uncertainties for the future. And one has to admit that an institution that has gone on for more than forty years must have acquired some middle-age spread, which it can well shed in the interest of greater efficiency.

Nothing is forever; and a more favorable conjuncture for international economic cooperation will surely emerge, if it is not already emerging. What can the World Bank and its supporters do to ride out the present rough weather and turn the ship around so that once again it becomes a significant provider of net capital to developing countries on terms that do not stifle their growth? Is the Bank robust and self-confident enough to keep faith with the whole range of its disparate membership and yet devise instruments of support that can discriminate between one borrower and another along some rational lines that might induce the community of lenders to overcome their current shyness? These and other questions so pertinent to the near-term future of the Bank admit of no easy answers. But they still have to be addressed and addressed urgently, if only because there is a new broom at the Bank. Dr. de Vries, who has had a long and distinguished career at the Bank and the Fund and who understands both the aspirations of the developing world and the exigencies of international capital markets, could not have chosen a better time to give us the benefit of his vast experience in delineating some of the steps that could enable the Bank to continue its good work. Not everyone may agree with his views, and not all his recommendations may be practical. But there is no doubt they deserve and will command serious attention.

I. G. PATEL

January 1987
London School of Economics and Political Science

Acknowledgments

While writing this book, I had stimulating contacts with many former colleagues at the World Bank and with Edward M. Bernstein, Edward Fried, and Richard Goode of the Brookings Institution.

I benefited from suggestions on a March 1985 draft of the study by J. Burnham, then U.S. executive director at the World Bank; Sumner M. Rosen of Columbia University; and Basil G. Kavalsky, Margret C. Thalwitz, Frank R. Vogl, and D. Joseph Wood of the World Bank staff.

A second draft entitled "The Future of the World Bank" was distributed to many interested persons in early 1986 as a Brookings Discussion Paper in International Economics. I am very grateful to several friends who commented in detail on this policy paper and encouraged its publication. They are Isaiah Frank of the School of Advanced International Studies at the Johns Hopkins University; Richard Goode, guest scholar at the Brookings Institution; H. Robert Heller, then at the Bank of America; Andrew M. Kamarck, former director of the Economics Department and the Economic Development Institute of the World Bank; P.R. Narvekar of the International Monetary Fund; Sumner M. Rosen; and Frank R. Vogl.

Throughout all phases of my study I was fortunate to have many discussions with my wife, Margaret Garritsen de Vries, historian of the International Monetary Fund.

I express appreciation to Irving S. Friedman for encouraging me to complete the manuscript and for leading me to Andrew E. Rice, who, well versed in international development issues, has been a very understanding publisher. He and Jane Gold, senior editor of Seven Locks Press, worked hard to transform the earlier policy paper into a readable book, and I am very grateful to them.

Introduction

HARDLY ANYONE TODAY is satisfied with the performance of the global economy. Many industrial countries have not been able to maintain steady and vigorous growth in which all their people shared. At the same time, excessive external debts and domestic financial difficulties in many developing countries have depressed their growth as well, and the poorest countries, mostly in sub-Saharan Africa, have suffered unprecedented declines in output, exports, and living standards. Despite the need for more capital for development, its mobilization has been impeded both by the imbalance in the external payments positions of the industrial countries and by the problems of the debtor nations. Private banks have stopped lending to most developing countries. Even industrial nations with persistent surpluses, such as Japan, have not begun to invest a larger share of their savings in the developing countries.

Recovery of the global economy will require close coordination of macroeconomic policies among the industrial countries and collaboration between their public and private sectors, as well as policy reform in the developing countries. Toward this end, many observers have urged that the World Bank play a broader, more effective role.

Thus, in the fall of 1985, the U.S. administration (and many others) recognized that the lingering debt crisis required fresh action. It called for a growth-oriented strategy, with the mobilization of some $40 billion in additional financing over three years for the debtor countries and the adoption of new policies to set these countries free from internal constraints. This strategy, supported by both industrial and developing countries, envisages that the World Bank play a central part in the resolution of the debt crisis.

During the past fifteen years the Bank has grown enormously in its financial strength, lending, and complexity. In so doing, it has attracted criticism from both the left and the right, as well as from those who feel that it suffers from lethargy and that its very size has become an obstacle to efficiency.

Critics on the left charge that, in practice, aid to developing countries has become a new form of imperialism and that the policy conditions that the Bank imposes in its lending activities interfere unduly in the internal affairs of sovereign nations. These critics point also to the control of the Bank by the wealthy developed countries and assert that the poorer borrowing nations have too little voice in its decision-making processes.

From the right come entirely different criticisms. Here the critics charge that the Bank has been far too unresponsive to market forces in furthering economic development. Its lending practices, they assert, have fostered public rather that private enterprise in the developing countries and have paid scant attention to the political interests of the industrial countries.

I shall examine these criticisms in some detail elsewhere in this volume. My own view lies far from either extreme and takes the position that the Bank has, on the whole, performed remarkably well. Yet, as this book will argue, there are many ways in which the Bank could improve its performance. In so doing, it would not only better serve the developing countries that are the primary focus of its activities, but would also enlarge its contribution to the health of the entire world economy.

Most of what I have written here is based on the firsthand knowledge that I acquired as a member of the Bank's staff from 1955 to 1984. My work in the Bank, which was preceded by several years in the International Monetary Fund, engaged me in both lending operations and economic analysis. Although my activities were first concentrated on Latin America, later they embraced such worldwide topics as export policies, economic projections, creditworthiness analysis, and industrial development.

My years in the Bank left me with the simple but pervasive ideas that underlie this book. Among them are

• Capital investment fuels growth and development. But more important, in starting and sustaining development, countries must acquire know-how in specific social and economic activities, and they must pursue sound policies to mobilize and allocate resources, both financial and real.

• Market forces are essential to efficient development sustained over a period of years. But if unbridled—or relied on to excess—they can play havoc with the international economy and run against the interests of nations. Individual developing countries must protect themselves against severe fluctuations in the external economy, as, for example, in commodity prices, market demand, and interest rates. Moreover, countries must build up institutions that make market forces work by providing market information, training and schooling, agricultural extension, transport and agribusiness enterprises, and sane planning in the public sector.

• Alleviation of poverty, a critical objective of development management, is enhanced by a proper policy framework and by direct and broad action aimed at improving the productivity of less advantaged population groups.

• The core function of the World Bank is to use its lending and technical assistance to help countries, in their particular circumstances, acquire essential know-how in specific activities, such as education, irrigation, building a transport network, or financing small business. The Bank must also help identify correct development policies and assist in their implementation—again in the country's particular political, social, and economic circumstances.

• In all its activities the Bank must, of course, recognize that recipient countries are sovereign and that, in the end, they determine their own destiny. Underdevelopment is partially a state of mind: where people become committed to development and thus to altering their institutions and attitudes, their country will not long stay poor and underdeveloped. But they will still need all the help they can find, and the World Bank must stand ready to work with people so committed to assist them on their way to development.

1

The Critics
Of the World Bank

IN RECENT YEARS the World Bank has been subjected to a barrage of criticism from all parts of the political spectrum. Some critics believe that it has been insensitive to the political concerns of the developing countries, that it primarily represents the views of industrial countries, and that, in applying the lessons of its experience, it often acts as a new kind of imperialist. But other critics, who believe the World Bank should be more responsive to market forces in furthering economic development, argue that both in its lending practices and in its mobilization of finance, the Bank has been too detached from the private sector and from the political interests of the industrial countries.

These criticisms of the Bank have been part of even more widespread attacks on "foreign aid" from both the left and the right. Both groups of critics have made many valid observations and have, in fact, probably contributed to the greater effectiveness of foreign aid today. But many of their arguments do not apply to the World Bank and are actu-

1

ally out of tune with its origin, objectives, and present policies.

The "aid is imperialism" school argues that the Bank imposes too many conditions in its lending and that the borrowing nations have too little voice in the Bank's decision-making process.[1] These critics are correct that Bank staff has often underestimated the impact the Bank has on the local scene, especially in the smaller countries, and has sometimes been perceived as arrogant. As a public institution, however, the Bank must pursue particular development objectives—including poverty alleviation—within existing social structures, even though those structures sometimes obstruct efficient development. In actual practice, moreover, the Bank's public pronouncements have been sensitive to the feelings of the less developed countries (LDCs).

Given the World Bank's role in these countries, the demands for a greater LDC share in decision making are well founded and have, in fact, been acted upon. For a number of years, the Bank has sought to increase the representation of developing countries in its management and staff.[2] In 1984 and 1985, for example, about one-third of senior managers and two-thirds of young professionals entering the Bank were from developing countries, and one can expect staff from developing countries to play an increasing role in the Bank's work in the future. (But note that an increase in LDC representation on the staff is not in itself enough to make the Bank more effective. Crucial also are insight into and dedication to development, attributes that are not limited to citizens of poor countries.)

Representation on the Executive Board continues to be based on shares in the Bank's capital. This principle seems entirely appropriate, since finance is basic to the way in which the Bank carries out its responsibilities. What is important in practice is that operating and policy decisions are mostly made by consent and discussion—in which the representatives of the developing countries fully participate—and rarely by voting. This cooperative spirit fits in well with the improved structure of North-South relations envisaged in the report of the Brandt Commission.[3]

The advocates of market forces criticize the Bank on quite different grounds. In his early studies, P.T. Bauer, one of the leading market-oriented critics of aid,[4] discusses the often spectacular growth effects of commercial export development in West Africa and Malaysia. Based on his early experience, he makes extensive criticism of the ultimate ill effects of official aid and of how it works in practice. He views aid as an international transfer of wealth to governments—not to people and least of all to the poor—whose bureaucrats have learned the practice of aidsmanship, the art of living beyond one's means and at taxpayers' expense. Aid, according to Bauer, promotes a disastrous politicization of life in the developing countries. Aid also supports Western-type heavy industries rather than small firms using indigenous technology, whereas commercial contacts are more geared to local conditions. Further, Bauer argues, not only does aid prolong countries' dependence on official assistance, but its effectiveness has also been overstated and oversold. Aid contributes at best a small fraction of investment, and its benefits cannot exceed the avoided cost of borrowing from private markets. Thus, as he explains, if aid to India were equivalent to 3 percent of India's gross domestic product and the cost of private credits (alternative to aid) were 20 percent, the benefits of aid would be at best equivalent to only 0.6 percent of GDP. But what is worse, overstressing the role of government discourages private market development and actually curtails the flow of private capital.

Bauer's emphasis on the effectiveness of market forces is indeed confirmed by the results of two decades of World Bank research on economic incentives for industrial and agricultural development. The Bank's economists would agree with Bauer that many countries, in a desire to reduce dependence on one or a few export crops, unfortunately discouraged the very activities in which they had comparative advantage. The present state of Ghana's cocoa industry and Nigeria's oil palm and groundnut crops is sad evidence of such misdirected policy.

But many of Bauer's conclusions stem from a narrow spectrum of experience. More systematic efforts have recently been made to determine the effectiveness of aid. These more carefully documented studies show that most aid has helped countries to produce more and to attack the causes of low productivity and poverty, and, that although some aid efforts *have* failed, the failure rate is probably not higher than that of other complex public or private investment undertakings.[5]

Thus, in the seventies, many new projects in integrated rural and livestock development suffered from overdesign and did not allow for the basic human and social setting in which they had to work. Food aid often destroyed the incentives to produce. On the other hand, the financing of many infrastructure projects and services in health, training, and education (e.g., in Korea) helped lay the base for subsequent growth.

It is important that right lessons about aid be drawn from experience. Three conditions seem essential for it to succeed. The first is a policy framework stressing the right combination of macro- and microeconomic measures; these include encouragement of domestic savings, exports, and output through a realistic exchange rate; positive real interest rates; and, generally, pricing policies that promote rational allocation of real and financial resources. The second is a *long-term* commitment to this framework and to the pursuit of the objectives of individual programs. And the third is a strong interest in development on the part of both government and business.

Moreover, little of the criticism of foreign aid by Bauer

and others applies to the World Bank, either as it was originally designed or as it operates today, although this is not to say that the Bank has not had project failures or that it has always laid sufficient stress on correct policies in specific country situations.[6] While it is true that the Bank often works closely with bilaterial aid agencies, especially in its coordination and cofinancing operations, World Bank operations are—and should be—distinct from bilateral foreign aid. In contrast to much bilateral aid, World Bank loans have *always* been designed to meet sound banking standards: they are expected to be repaid, and the record shows that they always have been. Bank loan conditions presume, or help establish, efficient policies regardless of domestic political considerations, and Bank lending operations are based on specific projects and programs that may take years to put in place.* Such conditions often cannot be applied by governmental bilateral foreign aid because much of its administration and orientation is subject to political change in the donor country. Further, some of the bilateral aid agencies lack the World Bank's experience in project design and execution, and they cannot be as objective, forceful, and persistent in policy dialogue. And in some major industrial countries (e.g., the United States and France), bilateral aid gets mixed up with security and military objectives. Thus, the difference between World Bank lending and foreign aid is more than semantics.

The following specific points further illustrate how the criticisms of Bauer and others simply do not apply to the World Bank:

- Many Bank loans are made not to governments but to decentralized agencies or enterprises. The Bank aims to have its loan funds administered and managed by

---

* Where policy performance has been particularly bad, the Bank has stopped lending or severely reduced new loan commitments, as it did during the later seventies in Ghana.

autonomous entities that are directly responsible for the execution of the project or the program. A basic operations procedure is to organize or set up an agency or autonomous institution capable of operating the project on a nonpolitical and businesslike basis (see chap. 6).

• Most Bank lending carries with it conditions on pricing and on businesslike behavior in the use of funds; user charges on public services are expected to cover the cost of the project and produce a reasonable return on the investment.

• While much World Bank lending for industry has indeed been concentrated in heavy manufacturing such as petrochemical, fertilizer, and metal processing, a substantial share of industrial lending has been channeled through local development banks, which relend most of the funds to medium and small firms in the private sector; and since the seventies the Bank has increased lending for small, labor-intensive industries.

• Although the Bank has stressed the importance of rational planning of government budgets and of public investment expenditures in particular, it has distinctly *not* encouraged command-type central planning. Rather, it has sought to encourage *decentralized* planning aimed at sensible decision making in individual sectors.[7]

• The projects for which the Bank lends show a high rate of return—an average of about 18 percent.[8] This does not deny that, as discussed in chapter 6, return on some projects is well below desirable levels, but the average rate of return is above both the cost of capital in recipient countries and the cost of commercial borrowing. Although this may puzzle theoretical observers with little familiarity of Bank operations,[9] the World Bank is able to achieve such high returns because it has long experience in searching out good projects and advising countries on them; it is willing to spend considerable effort and time in preparing such projects, often considerably more than commercial banks can afford.

Yet where commercial banks are willing to lend, the Bank generally does not displace them. Indeed, it makes its expertise available to them or helps arrange cofinancing with them for projects with high priority and high returns.

- The Bank's lending targeted at the poorer strata of the population increased from 5 percent of total in 1968–70 to 29.5 percent in 1979–81. While this lending did not constitute a "transfer of wealth" from the rich to the poor, as claimed by Melvyn Krauss and others,[10] it was designed to benefit the poor, who suffer most and hold back development. These loans aimed at improving the productivity of the poor through investment in irrigation, water conservation, and basic services (e.g., agricultural extension, research, and training); and although some projects did not attain their goals, the loans for rural development generally had a high investment return (20 percent as calculated upon project completion) and achieved a substantial improvement in per capita production and income of small farmers.[11]

In short, few of the often heard charges against the World Bank from the left and from the right stand up in the light of the Bank's record. Yet a review of this record in the following chapters does suggest that there are significant ways in which Bank policy and practice can be improved. These improvements, which would enable the Bank to play a broader, more active role in the international economy, are presented also in the pages that follow.

2

The World Bank Family: A Retrospective Look

OWNED BY MORE than 130 nations—not yet including the Soviet Union—the World Bank Group is a family of institutions of which the International Bank for Reconstruction and Development (IBRD), the International Development Association (IDA), and the International Finance Corporation (IFC) are the best known. All three lend to promote economic development—in 1986 a total of $17.5 billion, of which $13.2 billion was by the IBRD, $3.1 billion by IDA, and $1.2 billion by the IFC. (See table 1 for operating data.)

The origin of the IBRD goes back to the July 1944 United Nations Monetary and Financial Conference held in Bretton Woods, N.H., which also set up the Bank's twin, the International Monetary Fund (IMF).[1] IDA was organized in 1956 to provide assistance to the weakest and poorest of the developing countries. Four years later, the IFC was established to help finance private enterprise.

The basic strength of the Bank rests on the scope and flexibility of its charter, the Articles of Agreement, which emerged from the Bretton Woods Conference. The Bank's original design was—and still is—simple and effective: it was set up to be a highly efficient intermediary for the transfer of resources at the global level. Governments were to commit capital to the Bank, although only a small portion would be paid in. Most of the capital would remain on call, as a guarantee for the Bank's bonds. These bonds, to be sold in markets around the world, would be the main source of the Bank's finance. The Bank's objectives were broad; in the words of the Articles of Agreement, they were to finance reconstruction, to promote foreign investment and international trade, and to guarantee lending by others, or to lend itself, for the "more useful and urgent projects."[2]

Today, the IBRD and IDA are administered as a single institution, commonly called the World Bank.* All loans by both bodies are made either to governments or to entities with the guarantee of their governments, such as autonomous public agencies or domestic development banks. But the terms of these loans—their repayment period and interest cost—differ greatly between the two institutions and reflect their different sources of finance.

As already noted, the IBRD obtains most of its funds from selling bonds in the capital markets of the industrial countries. These bonds are backed by the capital put up or pledged by member governments, plus the Bank's accumulated reserves. Together these totaled $82.4 billion in June 1986. IDA, on the other hand, gets its funds by means of recurring cash contributions from governments, mostly from those of the industrial countries.

IBRD loans typically must be repaid over ten to fifteen years, and carry interest rates that reflect the rates the IBRD

---

* In this book, *World Bank* means the IBRD and IDA, except where either is mentioned separately.

pays on the bonds it currently issues in the market; in 1986 they carried an interest rate of 8.5 percent. IDA loans, or "credits" as they are normally called, have a repayment period of fifty years and carry an interest rate ("service charge") of only 0.75 percent, while in the first ten years no repayments are made at all. These IDA terms are clearly "concessionary"—that is, they are much softer than those prevailing in the market.

Both IBRD and IDA loans are for specific projects or carefully defined "programs," and both institutions apply the same standards of loan preparation and implementation. But IDA lends only to the poorest countries—those with per capita income below $730.

This income criterion includes many sub-Saharan African countries, as well as the two largest developing countries, India and China. In practice, IDA currently lends most of its funds (90 percent) to countries with per capita income below $400, such as Bangladesh ($130), China ($290), and India ($260).* Countries with per capita income above $730, such as Brazil ($1,890), Thailand ($810), and Turkey ($1,230), borrow from the IBRD. As countries gain in economic strength they "graduate" from IDA to the IBRD; several countries receive a blend of loans from both institutions. Eventually, when a country's per capita income exceeds $2,850, the IBRD itself gradually phases out its lending.

The International Finance Corporation is the World Bank affiliate that makes loans and equity investments without the guarantee of the recipient government. It shares many services with the World Bank and has access to the Bank's economic analyses. In addition, it has the same president as the Bank, and Bank executive directors (representing member governments) are also IFC directors. But even

---

* The per capita income figures are from the World Bank *Atlas* (1985). This is one of the Bank's most popular publications, initiated in the early 1960s.

though its operations overlap with the World Bank in lending for industry, the IFC is run as a separate institution. In 1985 it embarked on a five-year expansion program, which projects real growth in lending at 7 percent per year. To help finance this program, IFC capital is being doubled from $650 million to $1.3 billion.

Over the years, the Bank has managed its affairs in a businesslike manner. It has never suffered a default on its loans, nor has it had to call on any part of its capital to back its bonds, which have the highest credit rating. The Bank's operating figures (table 1) confirm a record of vigorous growth over the past two decades.

During these two decades—and indeed throughout the Bank's history—the international community has been fortunate in having had exceptionally capable management at the World Bank. The succession of able chief executives does much credit to the U.S. government, which, as the largest shareholder, has led in the search for leadership.[3] By agreement among the shareholders, all presidents so far have been from the United States, although this is a convention that may well now have become outmoded.

After the initial years, Eugene R. Black took the helm at the Bank in 1949 and, like Robert S. McNamara after him, remained for thirteen years. Black, who began his career in private banking, helped establish the Bank's operating procedures and defined the role of the executive directors in guiding policy and approving individual loan proposals put forward by management. He built the Bank's credit and credibility, opening markets for its bonds. During his tenure, the Bank developed the essential concept of the project loan, which enabled it to meet private market tests of sound finance. Under his guidance, the Bank took initiative on major multinational projects, of which the development of water resources in the Indus River Basin, on the border of India and Pakistan, was the most spectacular.

During most of his administration, Black was ably assisted

Table 1

Operations of the World Bank and IFC[1] (1965–86) (millions of U.S. dollars)

	1965	1975	1984	1985	1986
Subscribed Capital and					
General Reserves ...	22,564	32,430	59,461	62,573	82,444
Total New Borrowings ..	598	3,510	9,831	11,086	10,609
Net Income	137	275	600	1,137	1,243
IBRD					
Loan Commitments	1,023	4,320	11,949	11,358	13,179
Disbursements	606	1,995	8,580	8,645	8,263
IDA					
Credit Amount	309	1,576	3,575	3,028	3,140
Disbursements	222	1,026	2,524	2,491	3,155
IBRD & IDA					
Commitments	1,332	5,896	15,524	14,386	16,319
Operations Approved					
(number)	58	190	235	236	228
Higher Level Staff					
(number)[3]	532	1,883	2,735	2,800	3,617
IFC					
Investments Held	96[2]	779	1,990	2,116	2,387
Paid-in Capital and					
Accumulated Earnings	123	186	774	804	886
Net Income	4	8	26	28	25

[1] In this table and elsewhere in this study years shown are fiscal years ending June 30.

[2] FY 1966.

[3] In 1986 the World Bank's definition of higher level staff expanded as a result of job regrading.

Source: Annual Reports, The World Bank and IFC

by Robert L. Garner, who also became the first president of the IFC (1956–61). Unique in the Bank's history in that he came from private manufacturing industry, Garner made sure that Bank operations and loan projects were consistent with sound business principles.

George D. Woods (1963–68), an innovative investment banker from New York, started a critical process of attuning the Bank more closely to the changing needs of the developing countries. His initiatives and contributions were many. In spite of opposition from some members of the U.S. Congress, he broadened the base of support for IDA, which had come into existence during the Black administration. He initiated a more international process of assessing development issues (which subsequently resulted in the commission headed by Lester B. Pearson of Canada); he considerably expanded the Bank's efforts to coordinate long-term capital flows, especially to Latin America; and he established more effective relations with the United Nations and its other specialized agencies.[4]

Woods also started a rapid buildup of the Bank's economic work, even though he did not always apply economic policy analysis to lending decisions. During his term the Bank conducted in-depth studies of Brazil and India that helped reorient major lending programs in these countries. It learned how to finance development even under the inflationary conditions that were prevalent in Brazil, and although its recommendations on overall policies in India were subject to criticism, they eventually had a large payoff. Under Wood's leadership, too, the Bank deepened its understanding of the role of external debt in economic growth and started its work on African development.[5] And it was Woods who began the process of extending Bank lending beyond large-scale infrastructure to such new fields as small-scale agriculture, education, and water supply.

The World Bank greatly benefited from Robert S. McNamara's ability to lead and change large organizations (1968–81).[6] He was uniquely qualified to give the strong direction the Bank needed to adapt to new conditions. McNamara had a rare rapport with the leaders and thinkers of the developing world and a sense of identification with socioeconomic change; at the same time, he was able to deal with the often adverse political pressures that continuously buffet the Bank. He further extended the Bank's objectives well beyond the development of physical capital into the formation of human capital through programs for education, training, health, and nutrition. He deepened the Bank's concern with population pressure, with social and economic inequality, and with the means of improving productivity on which poverty alleviation must be based. Bank lending that aimed at improving productivity of the poorest groups increased from 5 percent of total in 1968–70 to 29.5 percent of a much larger total in 1979–81.[7] While McNamara recognized the industrial ambitions of the developing countries and increased the flow of finance for large-scale industry, he also stressed the importance of small industry. In the process of change and adaptation, he greatly increased the Bank's operations and staff, yet never lost sight of needed improvements in management and quality. During the years of the McNamara administration, total lending commitments increased thirteen times, the number of operations four times, and staff threefold.

McNamara showed less interest in macroeconomic issues, such as fiscal policies and the management of public investment. Instead, the Bank's dialogue with member countries in the seventies emphasized social and economic equity. But this emphasis, as well as substantial increases in private lending to the developing countries, rendered the Bank less influential both on efficiency in public investment and on improvements, often badly needed, in economic policies. Moreover, the greater complexity of the Bank's organization under McNamara and its increased paperwork meant that, under the less-centralized direction of his successor, its bureaucracy became an obstacle to its own effectiveness.

A.W. (Tom) Clausen (1981–86) had a more relaxed and decentralized style than his predecessor. During his tenure the Bank further adapted to changes in the international environment. In his first address to the Bank's Board of

Governors in September 1981, Clausen stressed the importance of agriculture and energy, and singled out Africa for
central attention. The Bank did indeed give priority to these
three areas and developed a program for sub-Saharan Africa
that was timely and well conceived.

But as many countries came to suffer from the effects of
the 1980–82 recession and the debt crisis, the Bank had to
face new tasks not foreseen in Clausen's initial speech:
restructuring the middle-income countries and initiating
diverse measures for coping with the excessive indebtedness
of several major borrowing members. Even though the Bank
had given considerable attention to external debt management in earlier years, it was sluggish in recognizing the importance of the debt crisis and only slowly adapted its operations. It did accelerate its loan disbursements to major debtor
nations from 1983 onward, but by mid-1985, three years
after the start of the debt crisis, it still had not put forward
a comprehensive strategy for addressing the problems of the
major debtor nations.

With his own experience as head of the Bank of America,
Clausen sought to increase cofinancing with private banks
and introduced new ways of raising finance for Bank lending. Still, by the end of his term, there remained much the
Bank could do to better adapt the design and terms of its
lending to market conditions and thereby encourage participation by private sources in the financing of Bank
projects.

From the very start of his administration, Clausen
understood that the Bank had to formulate its views on
development policy by integrating its analyses and recommendations on individual projects into a coherent whole—
the country program. He encouraged staff to engage in policy
discussions. But, unlike his counterpart at the IMF, Jacques
de Larosiére, he seldom involved himself in policy discussions with individual countries. Nevertheless, under his
management the Bank expanded policy-based lending,

which will continue to be important in coming years. In addition, Clausen presided over a systematic and comprehensive assessment of the Bank's future role. When he left in June 1986, the Bank had put together the various elements of a new agenda, but it remains for Clausen's successor to make the changes in procedures and organization needed to put the agenda into effect.

3

The Bank's Record

OVER THE YEARS, the World Bank has been able to blend analysis with operating experience in a unique way. Its strong financial and technical resources enable it to carry out its various functions with competence. Its diverse activities—research, finance, technical assistance, and economic advice—reinforce each other and, in the process, become more practical and realistic. When these activities are well managed, the whole of the Bank's impact is greater than the sum of its components.

To perform its tasks, the Bank has assembled a large, expert, and truly international staff. Its professionals today number 3,600, of which an increasing proportion comes from the developing countries. In addition, the Bank draws on the work of academic and research centers in both industrialized and developing countries. In fact, in analyzing new problems and recommending action, the Bank is able to assemble the necessary expertise on almost any development topic. Since 1978 it has published annual *World Development Reports* that have dealt with issues of central concern, such as rural development, structural adjustment, rational management of the public sector, population and health, and international capital movements. In so doing, it has retained its objectivity and has avoided taking sides on the North-South controversies that have beset many United Nations forums.

In addition to its global studies, the Bank carries on an extensive program of country-oriented economic research. Its economic reports on individual countries give advice on strategy and priorities and highlight important current issues such as how to

- improve the balance between the public and private sectors;
- constrain and rationalize urban growth, and encourage rural employment;
- recognize decreasing returns in large-scale industries, modernize and rehabilitate existing industries, and reduce import protection and discrimination against small, labor-intensive industries;
- increase the productivity and participation of women and the poorest population groups in all sectors of the economy; and
- restore domestic financial markets and institutions, and help in the recovery of the private sector and in the restructuring of industry and agriculture.

Much of the Bank's economic research cuts across countries and sectors. In the seventies it focused on rural and urban development, on small-scale agriculture and industry, on spreading the benefits of development to the poorest population strata, and on making social equity compatible with growth. At the same time, it extended its research on the structure and effects of price incentives for productive activities, which it had begun in the sixties. During this period, the Bank's research was ably managed by Hollis B. Chenery, who himself contributed to the comparative analysis of development patterns.

In the Clausen years, the Bank's research, under the direction of Anne O. Krueger, sharpened its attention to policy issues, with continuing emphasis on incentives (particularly for agriculture) and trade liberalization. It also initiated a study of government intervention and the interaction between adjustment and long-term growth.

By FY 1986, the Bank was spending $23 million on economic research and was a major center of development research. Despite this large expenditure, some important areas were neglected. For example, the Bank's research economists gave little help to developing a strategy for dealing with the debt crisis that emerged in 1982. Further, the research program did not pay adequate attention to the social effects of economic adjustment, a subject of key importance to present Bank operations, although to some extent the work of the Bank's Latin American division has made up for this lack.

Today the Bank faces a vast agenda of new research. Among the more crucial topics are the effectiveness of external assistance, new agricultural technology, the role of high-tech industries in low-income and semi-industrial countries, the social impact of the debt crisis, and the possibilities and impact of private-sector involvement in the development of Africa and other poor regions.

On the operational side, the Bank has acquired enormous experience in many economic sectors. Typically the Bank has been active in those sectors where help from private sources has not been available or where it could assist in preparing projects of interest to private finance. Bank lending and finance are of special importance in infrastructure and basic services—such as transportation—where private lenders and investors are often reluctant to make commitments but where public investment makes possible increased commodity production and exports. The Bank has helped achieve sizable savings for countries by working with them to improve the design of projects and to avoid excessive commitments and overinvestment. Indeed, in all its lending operations it has sought not merely to extend finance but also—and equally important—to provide the technical, financial, and economic advice that will make its lending most productive. This link between lending and technical and policy assistance is discussed in chapter 6.

The Bank's ability to adapt to changing conditions is manifest in its record. This becomes particularly clear in an examination of such key sectors as agriculture and rural development, energy, development banking, education, and health and population.

Agriculture and Rural Development

The World Bank has played a pivotal role in the global growth of agriculture that has occurred since the 1960s. The specter of worldwide food shortages, so feared a decade ago, no longer holds sway. Food output per capita has increased everywhere, except in sub-Saharan Africa. (Africa presents

Table 2

Composition of World Bank Lending Commitments

	1946–82		1983		1985		1986	
	$Billion	%	$Billion	%	$Billion	%	$Billion	%
Agriculture and Rural Development	26.5	25.2	3.7	25.5	3.8	26.1	4.8	29.3
Energy	20.2	19.2	2.8	19.3	3.6	24.9	3.0	18.5
Industry	19.6	18.6	2.5	17.2	1.9	13.1	2.5	15.6
Transportation	18.7	17.8	1.9	13.1	2.1	14.9	1.5	9.2
Non-project	7.2	6.8	1.4	9.6	0.6	4.4	1.3	8.1
Urban development	7.1	6.7	1.4	9.6	1.2	8.1	1.7	10.5
Education and Health	5.0	4.8	0.7	4.8	1.1	7.8	1.2	7.7
Technical Assistance	0.8	0.8	0.1	0.7	0.1	0.8	0.1	0.8
Total	105.2	100.0	14.5	100.0	14.4	100.0	16.3	100.0

Includes both IBRD and IDA. Fiscal years ending June. Industry includes basic industry, development finance companies, telecommunications and small scale enterprises. Urban development includes urbanization and water and severage. Technical assistance includes tourism in 1946–82 ($0.4 billion or 0.4 percent).

Source: Annual Reports of the World Bank.

a special problem, with food imports rising rapidly in recent years.) In China, India, and the major debtor nations, agriculture has been particularly dynamic.[1]

Research and new technology have been the driving forces of agricultural growth, especially in the development of high-yielding varieties of rice and wheat. The World Bank's contributions have been manifold: financing of high-priority investment components, combined with strengthening of policies and institutions, and widening of support for research essential to the developing countries. It has also played a key role in devising agricultural strategies. IDA has been closely associated with the self-sufficiency in food achieved by India.

Recognizing the key role of research, McNamara initiated a grant program and established the Consultative Group for International Agricultural Research (CGIAR) in 1971. The group is cosponsored by the Food and Agriculture Organization (FAO) and the United Nations Development Programme (UNDP). By 1981 the Bank had contributed $55 million in grants, 9.5 percent of total contributions to CGIAR.[2] Since then CGIAR's activities have expanded, with particular attention being given to improving African agriculture. Four CGIAR research centers are located in Africa, and all centers have growing outreach programs there.[3] In January 1985, CGIAR called a meeting to consider new initiatives for solving Africa's food problems, and in that year, thirty-eight donor members of CGIAR contributed $175 million, of which $28 million was given by the World Bank.

The Bank's lending for agriculture in the sixties had but weak operational links with "policy conditions." In its pragmatic approach—for example, in irrigation—it first concentrated on building infrastructure and physical plant. Once an irrigation system was in place, it could start linking its operation with the pricing of water and other "inputs" such as fertilizer and seed. Although such a realistic but gradual approach takes time, it pays off handsomely, as is evident in India and other countries.

Bank lending for agriculture and rural development added up to $34 billion during 1974–84 for projects that drew a total investment of between $90 to $100 billion. In 1983–85, such lending averaged $3.6 billion per year. Including loans for rural investments, agriculture-related lending exceeded 30 percent of total lending in those three years.

The Bank is in a strong position to assist in the continuation of agricultural growth, extending it to the poorest countries in Africa and elsewhere, upgrading technology, and increasing areas of cultivation. It has had a deepening involvement in improving agricultural incentive policies, crucial everywhere in the wake of the 1980–82 recession and now especially important in Africa since the decline in Africa's food output can be traced in part to adverse farm incentives. Bank lending for inputs into agriculture must now be combined increasingly with critical policy improvements. It is, of course, essential that action on agricultural incentives be integrated with overall incentives; protection of manufacturing penalizes agriculture.

New infrastructure, especially transport and communications, is also vital for continued agricultural growth everywhere, and especially in China and India, where the agricultural sector must still be integrated with the rest of the economy. Development of the North China plains could require billions of dollars in new construction. In low-income Asia, the Bank can be instrumental in resolving riparian rights and paving the way for the development of major river systems (e.g., the Ganges, Brahmaputra, and Mekong), all traversing areas of deep poverty. The development of the Indus River Basin, a major aspect of Bank operations in the sixties, set a solid example of what can be achieved in this area.[4]

In the middle-income countries, new investments are needed for increasing the value of agricultural production through improved processing, retailing, and marketing. These countries could be on the verge of reducing their agricultural work force through increased capital intensity and urban migration.

The Bank intends to pay greater attention to combating deforestation. (Lending for reforestation is projected to double in 1986–88 over what was spent in the prior three-year span, when it amounted to $105 million.) In many countries, the physical environment has been degraded at an unprecedented rate. Soil productivity has deteriorated through overcultivation and overgrazing on marginal lands and in forests. Africa's forests have been cut in half during this century, and the rate of destruction is accelerating. Hence, ecological degradation should be reversed through reforestation, conservation, land-use projects, and forest management incentives. Incentives directed at getting people involved in land conservation are needed not merely for modernizing agriculture but also for protecting and repairing the environment.[5]

The Bank's concern with deforestation in Africa reflects an increased interest in environmental issues. Somewhat belatedly, it has started to attend to the environmental consequences of its projects, such as those in large industry and resettlement. For almost two decades, the Bank, in cooperation with other agencies, has participated in the program to eradicate river blindness in West Africa and to redevelop the stream valleys deserted as a result of this disease. Its recent concern with wildland management, the destruction of tropical hardwood forests, and the adverse effects of large-scale hydroelectric projects is clearly overdue. It has also started to evaluate the environmental effects of its operations through economic studies of particular sectors, preparation of a data base on environmental problems, and evaluation of the effects of pesticides.[6]

In all, Bank lending may have to be stepped up if it is to help increase sound investment in agriculture. And there is scope for greater collaboration with private agricultural firms since, besides finance, private companies provide a wide range of services and marketing experience (shipping, insurance, information, and brokerage).

Energy

The quadrupling of oil prices in 1973 severely strained the balance of payments of oil-importing LDCs, who had to make basic structural adjustments in their economies, including more realistic energy pricing and increased energy production. The Bank accepted the challenge of the oil shock with innovation and flexibility. After taking stock of production and balance-of-payments prospects, it concluded that substantial new energy investments were needed. While it had long lent for electric power and coal development, the Bank entered the new areas of oil and gas development and promotion of conditions for exploration. In the process, its staff had to get acquainted with the private oil industry. Some private companies first met the Bank's initiative with skepticism and reservation, but many came to judge its staff work and operations as thorough and professional.

Ten years after the first oil shock, Bank lending for all forms of energy investment reached $3.4 billion, or almost 26 percent of total, compared with 15 percent during 1976–78.[7] Since 1984 energy lending has continued to increase apace with all other lending.[8]

As with all long-range sector programs, the Bank's energy activities were pursued with strong support from the industrial countries; the 1978 Economic Summit, for example, invited the Bank to start assisting in LDC oil and gas exploration. The Bank had learned the urgency of establishing preconditions for exploration and development, conservation, and investment in renewable resources. Natural gas proved to be more promising than had been envisaged originally. However, the Bank's proposal for a $25 billion energy affiliate was not accepted, primarily because of the large new financing required and the perceived competition with private companies.

The viewpoint of some private oil companies was clearly articulated by Fred C. Hartley of Union Oil Co. at a 1982 conference on the future role of the World Bank that was organized by the Brookings Institution: "The Bank has gone too far in its energy program. Oil and gas investment, from seismic work to exploratory drilling to development, should be the responsibility of the private sector, which has the skills and the capacity to do the job."[9] But Hartley added that the Bank can play an important role in financing infrastructure tied to oil and gas (including pipelines) *and* in offering insurance against political risk. This was also the view of the U.S. administration after 1980, which objected to several oil and gas projects in the state sector mainly on the grounds that private industry and finance could do the job and that, in any case, it was unwise to finance high-risk exploration with long-term debt. After 1984 the Bank became more restrictive in lending for state-sector oil and gas development.

Like many others in the energy business, the Bank assumed that energy prices would continue to be high well into the nineties and that, consequently, it had to support LDCs in taking long-term action to restrict demand and develop new supplies. Its basic objective was thus to assist countries in their post-1973 restructuring, exploiting their energy resources through more effective strategies and better resource use. It proceeded with an Energy Assessment Program, financed by UNDP, which analyzed energy policies and prospects and recommendedi essential steps for pre-investment or investment in some seventy countries. In so doing, it placed special emphasis on more rational pricing, thus encouraging changes in the level and pattern of demand and augmenting resources available for new investment.

The Bank's main role, however, was to act as a catalyst

both in mobilizing official and commercial finance, and in attracting private equity and expertise from international industry sources. It sought to act as an honest broker between the recipient country and the international oil companies and other souces of private finance. Indeed, it sought to keep its own financing to a minimum compatible with the objectives of essential policy and institutional improvement and maximum private cofinancing.

The Bank consistently found that developing countries had to step up their investment substantially and exploit their own energy potential more economically. Energy consumption in developing countries tended to rise faster than in industrial countries, but so had energy production. Consequently, if proper policies were pursued, net oil imports could rise by only 2 percent per year in the decade ahead as against 6 percent in the seventies. But to realize this potential, the Bank argued, the developing countries would have to double their investment in relation to GDP—to 4 percent—averaging $130 billion per year in the next ten years, with foreign exchange requirements of $50 billion. Two thirds of the investment would take place in the poorest countries and the oil-importing countries. This scenario represented investments needed to realize economic production potentials over the medium term. Investments of such magnitude would have to be accompanied by appropriate policies in the energy and other sectors. The economic justification of new energy investments had, of course, to be re-evaluated in light of the sharp decline in oil prices since 1984.

The very large investment possibilities foreseen stress the importance of mobilizing private finance, especially where the risk of failure is great. Private international oil companies have the resources to spread risks geographically and possess the latest technology. Further, they are the preferred source of risk capital and can facilitate the mobilization of loan capital. Hence, in the essential increase in LDCs' exploration activities, private oil companies have to play a key role. In recent years, however, they have undertaken only 25 percent of exploration in LDCs. Many situations are unattractive to private companies for a variety of reasons—for example, the small size or remoteness of the fields, the absence of exports (where the domestic market is small), or uncertain political and economic prospects. The Bank has sought to improve conditions for exploration by the private sector, where necessary through joint ventures. It can maintain a presence during exploration, reducing the perception of political risks. And in line with its policy to supplement rather than supplant private activity, it lends to national oil companies only when the projects are clearly economic and well managed and when private capital is not interested. Actually a wide range of countries can already boast of having well-managed national companies.[10]

Through 1980–85, the Bank lent for exploration promotion—establishing conditions in which private capital can start—by mobilizing data, strengthening management of local agencies, and improving policies.

By 1985, half the Bank's oil projects were for energy exploration; most were relatively small, and together they accounted for 11 percent of oil and gas lending. Many of the exploration projects have since led to discoveries or confirmation of earlier indications of deposits;[11] some have resulted in agreements with private oil companies.[12] In all, the Bank's energy program was a good example of flexibility, aiming at efficient development and improved cooperation with the private sector.

The collapse of oil prices in early 1986 brought them down to levels, in real terms, lower than at any time since the early forties. By mid-year, the World Bank had begun to reassess its own energy lending and policy advice. Many countries will have to reappraise whether their energy investments are economic at the lower prices that mpst experts now expect to prevail for some years. In this process the more rational pricing procedures adopted by many countries will continue to be welcome and essential. Reappraisal is critical in both oil-importing countries—for example, Brazil's massive gasohol program—and oil-exporting countries, many of which have tended to neglect non-oil activities—for example, Mexico and Nigeria.

Development Banking

Over the years the World Bank has lent some $11 billion to LDC development banks, assisting in new projects that had a total cost of $50 billion, mostly in small and medium private enterprises. To help spread the employment effects of these investments, an increasing proportion of this lending has, in recent years, been designed to support small, more labor-intensive industries. The Bank helped set up development banks, first as conduits for foreign exchange loans (as, e.g., in India and Pakistan) but increasingly as instruments for mobilizing finance and channeling it to high-priority investments. The Bank's policies toward these development banks set recognized standards for their operations and promoted the application of rational criteria for project appraisal. Besides using criteria for financial soundness such as debt-equity ratios and exposure limits, the Bank made a special effort to teach its many clients how to appraise projects economically.

Development banks are specialized banks offering long-term credits and sometimes making equity investments. They maintain close ties with their clients and often supply talent and management advice to both government agencies and the private sector. As they have grown in strength, an increasing number have been able to attract credits from private commercial banks, and some have been able to do without official loans (mostly in higher-income countries, such as Greece and Ireland). But with an increase in international commercial lending in the seventies, these banks encountered growing competition from foreign and domestic commercial banks, and in some countries they have experienced pressures from deregulation. Further, the 1980–82 recession and its aftermath have aggravated the financial problems of the development banks as even their best clients were unable to meet debt payments and many had to borrow to cover their interest and external debt obligations. At the same time, domestic financial markets—of which development banks are a part—have suffered from excessive interest rates, credit shortages, and fragmentation often caused by government policies.

Future World Bank lending to development banks (and other domestic banks) will have to go well beyond the institution building of the past. New loans can support improved financial-sector policies, the restructuring of promising enterprises and industries, and better performance in mobilizing domestic savings. In these efforts, the Bank will be able to draw on its experience in industrial finance as well as on its studies of the domestic financial sector and of industrial incentive policies. New financial sector lending could be particularly useful in its effort to expand policy-based lending.

Along with lending for industrial development, the Bank has made in-depth studies of the impact of price and fiscal policies on manufacturing industry operations. These studies began by analyzing the level and structure of import protection and its effect on the orientation and efficiency of industry—in particular, the extent of import-substitution and export promotion. They gradually extended to other forms of industrial incentives, such as fiscal exemptions and subsidies, location incentives, and special credits for capital investment. This painstaking work started some twenty years ago, first focusing on semi-industrial countries and more recently on Africa and other poor countries. The results of these studies have been a central feature in several comprehensive reports on industrial strategy and incentives in such countries as Brazil, Mexico, the Philippines, and

Turkey. Discussion of these reports has contributed to the policy rationalization process in these and other countries, making price and fiscal policies more efficient and responsive to market forces. The Bank continues to help initiate and support industrial incentive studies in a wide range of countries.[13]

Education

The financial crisis in many countries has strained education budgets at a time when popular demand for education is rising. There is now much greater stress on improved system management, efficiency, and mobilization of private finance.

In education as in other sectors there is also considerable differentiation among countries. In Africa, existing school systems have deteriorated, and the stress is on better use of available facilities. In India, there is scope for broadening elementary education and making more use of private training. China has set out to modernize all her educational facilities, especially in technical and higher education; with World Bank support she has successfully used television to expand engineering education rapidly and inexpensively. And in general, the middle-income countries can improve their research and development expenditures and their industrial training.

Though World Bank lending for education and training accounts for but 6 percent of its total lending, the Bank strongly emphasizes essential policy improvements in its operations.[14] It also seeks to enhance the contribution of private education and private support for educational expansion, while it increases attention to software, primary and adult education, and project-related training. The task ahead is large: fully one-third of children in LDCs are not yet enrolled in primary schools. But the benefits are also considerable; for example, it has been estimated that extension of four-year primary education can expand agricultural

output by 10 percent. Stress on education and system efficiency can have a direct impact on development
performance.

Health and Population

The World Bank has repeatedly drawn attention to the
economic and social consequences of rapid population
increase.[15] The developing economies are already severely
affected: witness the overcrowding of cities, the strain on
basic services, and the increasing imbalance between national
resources and population in the poorest regions. While rationalizing policies helps improve development performance,
population pressures can have adverse economic effects by
reducing national savings and the willingness to invest in
future development.[16] The Bank's projections strongly support the compelling case for population policies and research:

| | Population (in millions) | | |
	1982	2000	2050
China	1008	1196	1450
India	717	994	1513
Indonesia	153	212	330
Brazil	127	181	279
Mexico	73	109	182
Nigeria	91	169	471

Source: World Bank, World Development Report 1984, page 77.

Experience shows that family planning, when well conducted, can have strong community support, be culturally
acceptable, and produce results. After the success of family
planning assistance in East Asia and Indonesia, demand for
it is spreading to Latin America. Family assistance has been
effective in a wide range of conditions (as, e.g., in Mexico,
which experienced a decline in population growth from
3.2 percent in 1970 to 2.4 percent at present). Government

support has also been effective in India and parts of Bangladesh.

There is widespread need for more effective health services and family assistance: at present only 40 percent of couples in LDCs (other than China) have access to family planning services. Only 2 percent of official development assistance—some $500 million per year—is devoted to population assistance. This effort supports half of all family assistance costs outside China.

Population policy is an integral part of economic development, as is clear from the importance of reducing parents' dependence on children as a form of social security, of widening the economic opportunities of women, and of increasing women's access to education and other facilities.

The World Bank has lent support by focusing on the issues in population policy, reviewing necessary improvements in health facilities, and helping mobilize finance. Indeed, in this area it stresses that its prime contribution is through research dissemination and advice. Since 1980 it has committed $1.2 billion for population and health projects, many of which include assistance to family planning. In 1984, at the Mexico City International Population Conference, Clausen announced the Bank's intention to double lending for population and health programs in coming years. Lending for these sectors averaged $64 million in 1980–82 and reached $419 million in 1986. In the Bank's experience, effective programs offer a variety of family planning methods and information about them, provide basic health care aimed at improving maternal and child health, and have delivery services with outreach programs rooted in individual communities. Programs must be manageable and sensitive to religious convictions and cultural perceptions. The Bank has increasingly recognized the importance of nongovernmental organizations (NGOs) in population assistance. It encourages continuing support from NGOs, and in recent years it has increased cooperation with them.

4

The Changing
International Environment

THE WORLD BANK TODAY faces an international environment different in many ways from that which shaped the
Bank's policies and organization in the fifties and sixties.
Among the changes that have had profound implications
are (1) the dynamic increase in the role of private banks in
the financing of middle-income countries during the seventies, followed by the drastic reversal of their lending in the
eighties; (2) the worsening stagnation of the poorest countries and the consequent sharper differentiation among the
problems and performances of various LDCs;[1] and (3) the
realization that central government operations in many
LDCs must be made more efficient and brought into better balance with the private sector.

The Increased Role of Private Banks
The World Bank cannot isolate itself from the major
trends in international finance. Not only does it raise most

of its resources in capital markets, but it must attune its lending operations to those of other lenders and investors in developing countries. During the past decade and a half, this has meant taking account of the enhanced role of private commercial credit in financing LDCs during the 1970s, and then adjusting in turn to the sharp reduction in private bank financing that followed in the 1980s.

The figures are striking: in 1970 the share of private credit in total capital flows to LDCs was 26 percent; by 1981 it had risen to 41 percent, including bank credit, direct investment, and bond lending.[2] These private bank operations were heavily concentrated in the middle-income countries, with the poorer countries continuing to be predominantly dependent on official finance on terms softer than those the private banks were offering.

During the mid-eighties, the contribution of private banks dropped drastically in the wake of the 1982 external debt crisis. From 1981 to 1986 long-term lending by private sources fell by more than half (see table 3). However, when allowance is made for loan repayments and interest payments, the result was an actual *outflow* of resources of $11 billion in 1984 and $21 billion in 1985 (as against an inward transfer of $10 billion in 1980 and $9 billion in 1981).

In these difficult years the World Bank's lending made a strong contribution. The Bank's disbursements increased from $6.1 billion in 1981 to over $11 billion in 1984 and 1985, substantially rising as a share of total official lending to 38 percent. After loan repayments, the Bank's share of total net flows increased from 8 percent in 1981 to 20 percent in 1984 and 28 percent in 1985.

Overall, however, official long-term lending (by governments and multilateral agencies) to the developing countries stayed stable after the 1982 debt crisis. Thus there was no offset to the fall in private lending. New long-term lending from all sources, which had totaled $123 billion in 1981, dropped to $82 billion in 1985 and $72 billion in 1986.

Table 3

Long-Term Lending to Developing Countries (1975–86)[1] (U.S. $Billion)

	1975	1980	1981	1982	1983	1984	1985[2]	1986[2]
Gross Flows	43.8	102.8	122.8	115.8	96.5	88.3	81.7	72.0
Private[3]	28.9	74.6	91.3	83.9	63.8	56.1	52.1	41.0
Official	14.9	28.2	31.5	31.9	32.7	32.2	29.6	31.0
World Bank[4]	3.1	6.1	7.6	8.2	9.2	11.2	11.4	
% of official	20.7	21.6	24.1	25.7	28.1	34.8	38.2	
% of multilateral	72.1	54.5	63.3	56.2	60.5	67.8	67.7	
Net Flows	29.7	60.9	76.3	67.1	52.5	42.0	28.2	
Private	17.7	39.9	53.2	44.6	30.6	21.1	12.0	
Official	12.0	21.0	23.1	22.5	21.9	20.9	16.1	
World Bank[4]	2.7	5.1	6.2	7.4	7.9	8.3	7.8	
% of Total Net Flows	9.1	8.3	8.1	11.0	15.0	19.8	27.7	

[1] Flows are derived from disbursements of long-term loans to developing countries . Long-term loans have maturities exceeding one year. Net flows are gross flows minus loan repayments.

[2] 1985: preliminary; 1986: estimates.

[3] Data reflect rescheduling of short-term debt into longer maturities during 1983–85.

[4] World Bank includes IBRD and IDA

Source: World Bank data on long-term debt in *World Debt Tables 1986–87*, Abridged Version, Table 2 and pages 2-4 (Washington: World Bank, 1987).

Against these new loans were interest payments and principal repayments on older loans, so that on balance there was a net outflow from the developing countries of $26 billion in 1985 and $29 billion in 1986.*

The increase in lending by private banks during the seventies provided ample general purpose finance to the middle-income countries. The huge private credit flow was available for the financing of imports and government expenditures, and much of it was put to good use, judging by the favorable growth record of the borrowing countries in these years. But this ample finance came at a high cost. Overall the terms

* See *Developing Country Debt* (Washington: World Bank, 1987), xiii, table 2.

for the borrowing countries hardened considerably, in part because of the much shorter repayment periods of private loans compared with loans from official sources. Moreover, interest rates on private loans moved with current rates in the market, which rose substantially after 1979. The quicker repayment of private loans meant that, to achieve a net inflow of capital (i.e., net of repayment), borrowing countries had to contract much higher levels of new loans than before. This made borrowing countries more vulnerable to a decline in the demand for their exports or in the availability of new credit. As a result, when adverse conditions set in during 1980–82, the effect of the recession was particularly sharp in the major debtor countries, especially because the private banks had not normally made their lending conditional on the borrowing countries taking steps to achieve greater efficiency in private and public expenditures.

Even though private banks now have cut back their own credit flows, their operations and policies still have a major impact on the financial position of many LDCs. This is so because, for many of these countries, private banks are the most important creditors, accounting for 80 percent of the external debt of seventeen heavily indebted countries.[3] Moreover, in the absence of substantial new private lending, the reverse flow of interest payments to private banks significantly impairs the ability of countries to undertake new investments.

To attain a new and more vigorous growth momentum in the developing countries will be an arduous task. The LDCs will need to undertake extensive restructuring of their economies and make new investments; consequently, they will have to obtain new finance from all possible sources, domestic and external, private and official. Thus a strengthening of these countries' creditworthiness is paramount. Since private banks are now constrained in their new lending by portfolio considerations and by the large size of their investments in LDCs in relation to their capital, it will be up to the World Bank and other official lenders in the years immediately ahead to help restore LDC creditworthiness—and so lay the basis for increased private capital flows—through stepped-up official lending linked to policy improvements. As an immediate step, a larger proportion of the balance-of-payments surpluses of some industrial countries, particularly Japan, could be utilized for long-term capital investment in LDCs.

The World Bank has two functions in this situation. One is to encourage private lending and investment in LDCs by inducing policies in the borrowing countries that are more responsive to private lenders and investors and by associating the latter with the Bank's own operations (see chap. 7). The second is by stepping up its own lending.

In the exercise of these functions, the World Bank must, of course, maintain effective relations with both debtor countries and private banks. Further, it will have to display a keen sense of competitiveness in the pricing and conditions of its loans. Although it can render essential nonfinancial services in connection with its lending, countries will be reluctant to pay the price for these services if the cost of Bank loans is too high in relation to other finance available to the LDCs.

The Sharper Differentiation Among LDCs

A second major change in the international economy is the more marked differentiation among developing countries that has appeared during the seventies and eighties, as countries experienced deep shocks associated with changes in energy and basic commodity prices, the impact of the 1980–82 recession, and the ensuing debt crisis.

One group today, the oil-producing countries, is basically creditworthy—some indeed have become providers of capital to other LDCs—although needing technical assistance. A second group of middle-income, semi-industrialized countries, including Brazil, Mexico, Tunisia, and the Philippines, have built a new urban industrial base but now need to further restructure their economies. For this purpose, they require substantial external capital since their growth has been bogged down by adverse movements in commodity prices and by increased protectionist pressure in the industrial countries.

A third group, led by Korea and other Pacific Basin countries, has pursued more market-oriented policies and has been more successful in avoiding or overcoming the ill effects of excessive indebtedness and recession. These countries could become leaders in a new growth momentum and should be able to get most of their external capital from private sources.

Finally, there are the poorest countries, primarily in Africa, which have for many years been falling behind the rest of the world. They deserve special attention, both for humanitarian reasons and in the interest of a stronger and more stable international community. Fortunately, the largest of the poorest countries, China and India, have established a record of growth and financial stability in recent years. They are able to use large amounts of new external capital productively.

In realizing its objectives, the World Bank necessarily must respond to the needs of its borrowing members. Today, given the sharp differentiation among groups of countries in the wake of major changes in the international economy, the Bank will clearly have to play a distinctly different role in each group of countries.

Greater Reliance on Market Forces

A third major element in the international environment is the broader recognition, in both developing and developed countries, of the role of market forces in development. In most LDCs, government control and intervention were, until recently, decisive in many critical sectors, such as heavy manufacturing and mining, agricultural extension, credit and related policies, infrastructure, education, and other basic services. The private sector often was given a subsidiary role. But during the seventies, the public sector in many countries became overextended, often, curiously enough, with financial help from private foreign banks. Increased efficiency in the public sector—especially through improvements in domestic pricing and foreign exchange rate policies, in the quality of investment, and in the operations of state enterprises, which must be placed on a self-financing and more autonomous footing—is now often a critical element for further sustained development.

Even more important, the private sector, which has suffered badly from the excessive growth of the public sector, from the accompanying price and other distortions in the economy, and from the impact of the global recession and the debt crisis, must now be strongly encouraged. Recovery of private industry and finance is essential to any new agenda for more vigorous growth.

Challenges Facing the Bank

These changes in the international economy present the World Bank with challenges that are new in the history of development finance:

• Never before has the largest group of borrowers of the Bank—the principal debtor nations, mostly in the middle-income range and concentrated in Latin America—suffered from such severe difficulties in structural growth, domestic finances, and balance of payments. To meet these difficulties, the Bank needs to develop a concerted strategy that recognizes the common problems facing these borrowers.

• A large group of countries, mostly in sub-Saharan Africa, are suffering not merely stagnation but also absolute declines in living standards, production, and exports. Here the Bank must encourage both new domestic policies and more effective external assistance to reverse the present decline.

- In the past, the Bank often took the lead in project development and finance, and indeed often proceeded in a relatively independent fashion. But now it must recognize the much greater executive capacity of many LDCs and the important present or potential contributions of many other lenders. Increasingly, it must induce others to provide more finance for the recovery and restructuring of the major debtor countries.

- Much external finance has been provided on terms ill suited for investment projects and programs and for countries with wide fluctuations in foreign exchange earnings. Reform in financing terms and techniques is urgently needed. The World Bank will need to contribute to such improvement and innovation through its own lending practices and improved cofinancing with private lenders and investors.

To face up to these challenges, the Bank will need to continue reorienting its policies and procedures. Fortunately, in making the necessary changes, it can build on its strong record of adaptation to changing external circumstances and demands for its services.

5

Critical Issues
Facing the Bank

THE WORLD BANK'S role should be determined by the unique contributions it can make in areas of global concern. It is worthwhile to take a closer look, therefore, at three critical issues that seem especially to be within the Bank's sphere of interest: the plight of the poorest countries, the restructuring of the economies of the semi-industrial countries, and the recovery of the private sector in developing countries.

The Plight of the Poorest Countries

Many of the poorest countries have been falling farther and farther behind the other developing and industrial countries. In sub-Saharan Africa, for example, per capita income in 1985 was less than what it was in 1960. From 1980 to 1985 food output fell each year. Today Africa can satisfy only one-fifth of its cereal requirements. A large part of African industry stands idle because of depressed demand, poor design, and lack of imported raw materials and spare parts.[1]

Africa's predicament has come about despite generous levels of external assistance. On a per capita basis, it has been a prime recipient of official development assistance (ODA), the external finance provided by governments on concessionary terms in the form of grants or of credits with interest rates and repayment periods much more generous than those provided by the market. Thus, for Africa, ODA receipts per capita in 1970–82 increased by 5 percent per year in real terms, much faster than for other developing countries.[2] In 1982 ODA receipts per capita were $19 for all sub-Saharan Africa, and $46 for low-income, semiarid Africa, compared with only $5 for South Asia.

But the rapidly increasing aid flows covered a progressively smaller portion of the current account deficit of sub-Saharan Africa. For example, ODA to the oil-importing African countries increased from 2.7 percent of GDP in 1970 to 5 percent in 1980 (or from $1.6 billion to $4.3 billion in 1978 dollars). But the current account deficit increased more rapidly, from 2.4 percent of GDP to 9.2 percent. Thus, the increase in ODA covered less than half the increase in the current account deficit.

This growing deficit was not the result of a deterioration in the terms of trade, that is, the purchasing power of their exports. Per unit of exports, sub-Saharan Africa's terms of trade improved by 2.5 percent per year in 1970–79. But the volume of exports fell drastically. Excluding fuel, Africa's share of world exports dropped from 18.6 percent in 1970 to 9.2 percent at the end of the decade.[3]

The recession of 1980–82 in the industrial countries had a particularly severe impact on sub-Saharan Africa. It brought about a decline in the terms of trade, associated with the recession, that represented a loss of GDP of 2.4 percent for all the low-income countries in the region.

Reversing Africa's stagnation and decline will be a slow and long process, requiring a combination of improved domestic policies with more effective external assistance. In

1984 the World Bank recommended that total capital flows to sub-Saharan Africa over 1985–88 be maintained at the 1980–82 level of $11 billion, well above then current plans. In 1986 the Bank estimated that concessionary aid had to be increased by $2.5 billion per year in 1986–90 over planned levels, merely to restore Africa's import capacity per capita to the 1980–82 level. This calculation assumed a significant increase in exports plus enlarged aid flows resulting from special efforts of the European Community and operations of the Special Facility for Sub-Saharan Africa operated by the World Bank.

But in practice, actual absorption of productive external capital (as distinct from emergency aid) will depend on improvements in domestic policies and use of capital—incentives for greater efficiency by farmers and business in the use of capital, educational reform, expanded agricultural extension and research, and improved irrigation management. The need for these improvements is widely recognized. It is also reflected in the rather low percentage of World Bank commitments to Africa. They averaged only $1.9 billion per year in sub-Saharan Africa, less that 13 percent of total World Bank lending in 1983–85. Slow progress in program development was the principal factor underlying the Bank's poor commitment performance, which occurred despite a major shift of capable personnel to the Bank's African operations.

In addition to the offical assistance agencies, private voluntary organizations are making a cost-effective contribution in the poorest countries. Voluntary operations are of particular interest in strengthening community development, education, health, and agricultural extension. In financial terms, assistance from private agencies now exceeds $2 billion per year; in addition, more than $1 billion of official funds are channeled through them.[4] Recognizing that their efforts complement those of national governments and offical financial agencies, the World Bank is beginning to make greater use of such agencies in its own operations through more regular contacts and improved channels of information.[5]

In contrast to Africa, the prospects in the largest of the poorest countries, China and India, are much brighter. In both countries the World Bank is already playing a significant role in strengthening technological know-how in agriculture and industry, as well as in improving infrastructure and basic services. In recent years both countries have been placing more stress on rational economic incentives. The size of their capital requirements and the direction of their policies suggest that private banks and investors may be able to increase activity there. However, in practice, the inflow of private capital will be constrained by the countries' export performance and by the drag of large poverty-stricken regions on the more affluent sectors of their economies. Given these constraints, a high level of operations by the World Bank and other official lenders is particularly important.

Restructuring the Semi-Industrial Countries

Restructuring the middle-income countries is central to a new growth-oriented strategy, particularly in the major debtor nations of Latin America. It involves a wide range of long-term adjustments in the economy as a whole, as well as action in specific sectors such as manufacturing, agriculture, and infrastructure. Restructuring became urgent in the seventies as commodity prices—particularly in energy and basic metals—underwent significant shifts. Moreover, even outward-oriented countries had to upgrade and diversify their manufactured exports as a result of intensifying international competition and protectionist pressures. The crisis that began with Mexico's failure to meet her debt obligations in the summer of 1982 further emphasized the urgency and broad nature of the required restructuring.

The prospects for restructuring have been affected by the

declines in the U. S. dollar exchange rate, interest rates, and oil prices that have occurred since the fall of 1985. These declines have made possible the refinancing of outstanding debts at fixed or lower interest rates and the freeing of scarce foreign exchange resources for essential investments.

But the effects of international price changes are highly differentiated across countries. Favorable effects are offset by falling export prices for countries dependent on oil and other basic products. In a more competitive (and often more protectionist) world, developing countries have no alternative but to become more efficient through improved organization, domestic policies, new investments, and restructuring. In addition to a stronger export orientation, continued efforts are needed to place state enterprises on a more businesslike basis and autonomous footing, independent of budget support and responsive to market forces. Bloated public investment programs, recently squeezed to minimal levels in some countries, can be revitalized only in a rigorous process of determining priorities, in which the World Bank can be of special assistance. Some countries also need to improve their ability to maintain rational price incentives for industrial development.

External capital is critical to getting restructuring and new investment under way. New external finance may have to reach 10 to 15 percent of a rising level of investment, or about 2 to 3 percent of GDP. But amortization and interest payments on outstanding debts significantly reduce the level of finance available for investment and, indeed, have now turned a gross capital inflow into a net outflow of resources. The stretch-out of amortization under multiyear debt restructuring agreements in a number of countries has provided significant though temporary relief. But in practice the outflow of debt service payments may have to be reduced further as part of a growth-oriented strategy. Since disruption of debt service payments is hardly conducive to marshaling new resources for economic growth, any further steps that are taken should be in close collaboration, not confrontation, with creditors. Further, any changes introduced should be attuned with market forces, something that will be more possible and likely if interest rates continue to decline.

The medium-term projections published by various institutions in the wake of the 1982 debt crisis suggested that, under fairly plausible assumptions, most debtor countries would be able to manage their external debt obligations although at the cost of a sharp reduction in growth.[6] But by 1985 many of the assumptions underlying the projections proved too optimistic. The growth prospects of industrial countries, trends toward protectionism, and the cautious attitude of private banks did not favor an early restoration of the creditworthiness of many debtor countries. Further, the projections published by the IMF in 1984 and 1985 brought out some of the strains under which the major debtors labor. Their import growth has been constrained by the scarcity of foreign exchange earnings and finance, and this pressure on imports has been hard to manage in a time when these countries must orient themselves outward. Moreover, the essential restructuring of their economies will have to be undertaken while private bank credit is projected to grow more slowly—in some countries much more slowly—than domestic output and investment. This decline in private bank credit thus stresses the importance of contributions of private direct investment and long-term lending by the World Bank and the other multilateral development banks.[7] Over the longer term, one must assume that outward orientation in developing countries will tend to accelerate the growth of imports and external financing needs, and that these needs will be met by rising exports and capital inflows.

The export performance of the debtor countries must underlie the restoration of their creditworthiness. In countries experiencing debt servicing difficulties, exports are simply too low compared with their debt liabilities. This disparity reflects the fact that the integration of the international financial system outpaced the extent of trade expansion of the LDCs. If the major debtor countries are eventually to meet their debt obligations without write-offs and interest subsidies, they will have to increase their export sector markedly in relation to their domestic economy. The extent and significance of the necessary turnaround in export orientation may well have been understated in the export projections prepared by various institutions and scholars after 1982. It is noteworthy that in the seventies a major debtor like Brazil had a strong export performance—with manufactured exports rising by 23 percent per year and reaching half of total exports. But even after such strong growth, Brazil's export sector accounted for only 9 percent of her national economy in 1982, a small percentage roughly comparable with that of China and India, who relied to a much smaller extent on external capital. In contrast, South Korea's export sector accounts for 39 percent of her economy and her manufactured exports for 90 percent of total exports.[8] The small percentage for Brazil can be explained by the size of her economy, yet it is incompatible with the size of her debt.

Besides developing their exports, several countries will have to restore confidence in their private sectors and encourage repatriation of capital. Capital flight has been of major proportions in Venezuela, Argentina, Chile, Mexico, and the Philippines. World Bank data suggest that in some countries capital flight was equivalent to 50 to 100 percent of the increase in external debt in 1979-82.[9] Governments often induced capital flight by encouraging easily available loans from abroad and by making investment abroad more attractive than at home. The most important underlying factors were overvalued exchange rates and irrational conditions in domestic credit markets, both prime candidates for policy reform in a growth-oriented strategy. But the more favorable experience of Brazil, which suffered little capital flight, suggests that more is involved. In Brazil, the private sector has confidence in the future of the economy, a confidence to which effective administrative measures have contributed. Until recently this factor appeared to be lacking in Mexico, partly because of ineffective action against inflation, continued use of domestic controls, and the effects of the nationalization of private banks, all of which adversely affected business confidence.

Restructuring has a wide scope because of the many different measures that must be taken, the diversity of sectors affected, and the geographic spread of countries concerned. It is of central importance in Latin America, which, in the best of circumstances, will not regain its 1981 per capita income until the late eighties—a difficult and slow process. It also has top priority in Turkey, Yugoslavia, North Africa, and the Philippines. Several East Asian countries and Indonesia have already made a serious start in the restructuring process.

The World Bank can lend special support through technical assistance and policy-based lending to key institutions. It has already begun lending for rationalization of state enterprises and the restructuring of development banks and their economically viable industrial clients; these loans support new investment and can be linked to specific policy reform. In addition, through cofinancing and direct private-sector participation in its projects, the World Bank can play a strong catalytic role in attracting essential private support for restructuring (see chap. 7).[10]

The 1982–85 stabilization efforts of several countries have laid the basis for a resumption of growth in the remainder of the decade. The October 1985 initiative of U.S. Treasury Secretary Baker recognized that a viable strategy must combine domestic policies aimed at improving growth with an increase in net external capital from both private and official sources. Although changes in Turkish policies in 1981 showed what could be achieved in export growth and attracting new capital, they also underscored the difficulties of rationalizing state enterprises and domestic financial markets. In 1985 and 1986 a number of countries, notably Argentina and Brazil, took measures to reform the public sector, but these new programs and essential actions in other countries cannot prevail without sustained growth and new finance. In some of the more difficult country situations, it may be necessary to formulate concrete programs that combine stabilization and debt rescheduling with long-term restructuring and new finance.

Recovery of the Private Sector

The World Bank can play a more vital role in strengthening the private sector in developing countries. Private manufacturing and farming, as well as private savings and investment, have suffered severely from the impact of the 1980-82 recession, the debt crisis, high interest rates, and the overexpansion of the public sector. A well-organized and comprehensive effort is needed to strengthen the private sector, since no growth strategy is feasible without full support of private entrepreneurs and farmers who, together, contribute about three-fourths of GDP in most countries. Essential restoration of confidence and repatriation of capital are inconceivable without full participation of the private sector. Private entrepreneurs play a key role in making the economy more efficient and competitive.

The private sector is weakest in sub-Saharan Africa and other poor countries, where it is overprotected and heavily dependent on government assistance. In many countries it hardly exists except in the "informal" or "unofficial" sectors. Few Western countries could have built their own indigenous technology and capital base with the overwhelming government presence that exists today in most African countries.

Yet the position of the private sector is perhaps more

promising in some of the larger of these countries. Nigeria's private sector has large potential; with adequate policy support it can grow rapidly. India has a widespread and vigorous private sector ready to assume a much larger role in the economy. The government has started to give it greater freedom and encouragement, particularly in technologically advanced and export-oriented industries; on the whole, however, India's private sector still suffers from excessive regulation and restriction. The World Bank has quietly supported more market-oriented policies in India through project-specific technical assistance, through operational relations with development banks and industrial and transport enterprises, and through cooperative research. Continued action toward making the Indian economy more efficient and dynamic should pay off handsomely.

In the People's Republic of China, the government is transferring greater autonomy to small- and medium-size enterprise while giving *all* industry greater leeway in operations and investment decisions. All Chinese enterprises are expected to respond to consumer demand and to a more rational price structure. Although the transition from a loosely planned economy with numerous regulations and only notional pricing to one with rational price signals poses perplexing problems, the Chinese are meeting these problems pragmatically and are interested in learning from experience elsewhere.

The private sector is facing its greatest challenge in those middle-income countries that had to seek a rescheduling of their external debt. These countries entered the seventies with a private sector that had grown vigorously in the previous two decades. By the early seventies it had become clear that those countries fared best that stressed reliance on market forces, export orientation, and private initiative. But in the wake of the first oil shock, many countries adopted policies that, in effect, suppressed the private sector. They stressed what often were capital-intensive projects in the state sector and made excessive use of price subsidies, controls, and state finance. Foreign exchange controls tended to weaken business confidence and adversely affect operational efficiency. Governments put an excessive claim on available resources through their budget deficit (15 percent of GDP or higher in Brazil and Mexico) and through credit subsidies to preferred sectors. Domestic interest rates increased to 25 percent or more *above* inflation. Companies had to borrow to stave off bankruptcy, and little credit was available for new investment. Corporate distress of this kind was prevalent in several countries, including Argentina, Chile, Turkey, and Uruguay.

The World Bank has usually sought to provide adequate finance for private enterprise. In fact, most of its loans are for directly productive activities, via development finance companies or other credit programs and industries, or they indirectly support commodity production through transportation, training, or other services. In its urban development lending, the Bank encourages private companies in transport and basic services. In education, it emphasizes the effectiveness of private schools and the importance of private finance.

Although the Bank has usually been pragmatic in its dealings with the private sector, it has refrained from giving much explicit attention to private-sector development, and indeed, many outside observers find the Bank overwhelmingly biased toward the public sector. In fact, however, the Bank has advocated policies that encourage efficiency, stressing that these policies must be applied in *both* sectors. Further, it has shied away from advocating private ownership per se, lest it breach its own nonpolitical character. Many countries believe in state ownership of at least some industries. But inefficiency in the state sector may be a major obstacle to growth, and in many areas privatization will encourage efficiency and competitiveness, whereas public ownership may encourage intervention and excessive dependence on public finance. Applying principles of efficiency to public-sector services can be revolutionary and is always complex and difficult. These points are illustrated in a little-known 1982 World Bank publication, *Economic Development and the Private Sector.*[11]

The widespread and severe malaise in the private sector calls for a comprehensive strategy designed to remove present obstacles to more vigorous growth. Effective programs would necessarily have many elements:

• Changes in economic policies to make all productive enterprise more efficient. These changes would include less reliance on controls and subsidies, lower and more even protection against imports, and realistic exchange rates. Private-sector development is encouraged by a stable economic and business environment.

• A better balance between public- and private-sector activities. In many countries the public sector has been overextended and often has entered activities that now can be undertaken better by private business, while economic policies have tended to be unfair to private industry, particularly small- and medium-size enterprises. Up to now, allocation of credit has strongly favored state enterprises in most countries.

• Restructuring of state enterprises and placing them on their own feet financially, and reallocating real resources in favor of private, predominantly labor-intensive industries. Although the World Bank in recent years has lent for the restructuring of large state enterprises, as well as for the rehabilitation and development of specific industries such as textiles or steelmaking and fabrication,[12] these loans in some ways merely extend the Bank's industrial project lending of the sixties and seventies, which supported capital-intensive industrial development (e.g., in Brazil).[13] Revitalization of the private sector must go well beyond the restructuring of state industry.[14]

• Introduction of more rational credit policies, eliminating credit allocation and interest rate subsidization. Major action is needed to put domestic development banks on a sound footing and to restructure many economically viable private enterprises that have suffered from corporate distress. The World Bank has made several studies of countries' financial sectors; these studies can be activated as a basis for lending or as an integral part of broader reform programs.

• Assurance of adequate access to technological information, usually through private channels, which can serve the diverse needs of industry better than government agencies. The World Bank itself is an important source of technological information through advice and assistance on project development in many sectors and through the financing of education and training (see chap. 6).

• Improvement of infrastructure facilities that serve areas where export and other private industries can flourish.

The World Bank makes important contributions in each of these fields. But until 1986 it had not brought together these various elements into a unified, comprehensive program for private-sector development. On the other hand, its affiliate, the IFC, is in the midst of an expansion program, with operations projected to grow by 7 percent per annum. The IFC focuses on the mobilization of external finance for individual private enterprises, including the restructuring of enterprises to which it has lent in the past. In addition, it assists development of indigenous capital markets and undertakes studies of industrial investment incentives, although as an institution it has had limited influence on country policies.[15] But the IFC is run quite separately from the World Bank, and one gains the impression that, between the Bank and the IFC, comprehensive action on private-sector development has fallen between two stools, even though the urgency and importance of this topic warrant more intense collaboration, if not full integration, between the work of the two institutions. A like judgment was made fifteen years ago in the Mason-Asher volume, *The*

World Bank Since Bretton Woods.[16] It is noteworthy that up to 1986 little action had been taken toward achieving close integration of the private-sector policy work of the World Bank and the IFC.

6

Linking Bank Lending
With Policy Reform

WHEN THE WORLD BANK makes a loan, it normally gives much technical assistance and policy advice. Indeed, giving such advice is a central function of the Bank, as important, if not more so, than the transfer of finance. This is true whether a loan finances a single development project or is aimed at restructuring a range of economic activities.*

Traditionally, Bank loans have fallen into one of three categories, of which project loans are the most familiar. In

---

* Although this chapter deals primarily with policy advice, the significant role of technical assistance—in engineering, administration, financial management, etc.—should not be overlooked. Often, indeed, the technical assistance provided by the Bank determines the very nature of the project that the loan supports. The Bank's direct financing of technical assistance exceeded $1.3 billion in 1985; in addition, the Bank contributed $170 million to 117 projects for which it was the Executing Agency for the UNDP. These figures, of course, are only a fraction of the cost of the Bank's staff work on economic, sector, and project reports that are the backbone of all its technical help.

project loans, the borrower is usually an operating entity, such as an electric power company, a school system, or a manufacturing enterprise, although the recipient's government must guarantee repayment of the loan.[1] A second category of loans are those made to finance activities in a single economic sector or subsector—for example, energy conversion of a specific industry, irrigation works in a nationwide program, national distribution of electric power, or the planning of a road network combined with a two-year road building and maintenance program. Loans addressing problems in such specific sectors are called "sector investment and maintenance loans."

A third layer of lending cuts across several sectors and deals with such broad problems as management of a government's investment budget or its external debt. Such loans—known as "program or structural adjustment loans" (SALs)—are permitted under the Bank's charter under "exceptional circumstances."[2] Closely associated with these broader loans are quick disbursing loans made by the Bank in emergency situations, such as the 1978 loan to Nigeria to help in its post-civil war reconstruction.

In much of the discussion about World Bank operations, a distinction is made between project and nonproject lending. This distinction is essentially a legal one, based on the Articles of Agreement, but in practice and in substance it is unimportant. Instead, the critical issue is how the Bank can best deliver its policy and technical assistance—through narrowly or broadly conceived loan projects.

The answer depends on many factors, including a country's circumstances and the alternative financial resources available to it. But as a general rule, most of the Bank's lending has been—and most likely will continue to be—in the area where it has the greatest comparative advantage: the preparation, evaluation, and financing of specific investments in physical or human capital.

On the other hand, sector loans are appropriate in countries that have built up strong and effective agencies and institutions capable of dealing with problems and investments in particular sectors (electric power, various kinds of transport, education, etc.), as have many countries in East Asia and Latin America. In such countries, these institutions can and should administer sector loans, including loans for rehabilitation and maintenance, which are now particularly important in assuring the benefits of past investments.

Beyond these project and sector loans, however, the Bank since 1980 has made an increasing number of broad policy loans that have addressed essential reforms and supported investments needed to enhance the overall efficiency and competitiveness of economies and their adaptability to change in the external environment. In the seven years ending June 1986, the Bank lent a total of $11.2 billion for such structural adjustment, of which $5.3 billion were SALs and $5.9 billion were adjustment loans in specific sectors. Preparation of SALs and subsequent follow-up have included in-depth assessment of the policy changes needed to induce greater efficiency in the economy, as well as studies of individual sectors or industries, the public investment budget, and conditions in domestic credit markets. The essential feature of SALs is not their rapid disbursement (usually two years), which is most often mentioned in public discussion about the pros and cons of this type of lending; it is the major role they have played in introducing changes in policies with favorable effects on economic efficiency and on the planning and execution of long-term investments. Toward this end, SALs have often been combined with lending for more specific projects or sectors, such as for key industries and development banks, or for agricultural extension and credit.

For example, the 1980 and 1982 SALs to the Philippines supported the liberalization of policies that affected trade and industry (although this liberalization was later slowed down by the impact on the Philippine economy of capital flight, the external recession, and the political upheaval leading to the demise of the Marcos government). The first of these loans was preceded by an in-depth study leading to both an official statement on industrial development and strategy, and a program for modernizing manufacturing and rationalizing protection and industrial investment incentives.[3] It was envisaged that protection would be reduced in phases, with particular industries receiving finance for rehabilitation and technical assistance. At the same time, the Bank lent for reform of the banking system (the 1981 "APEX" loan), improvement in the system of finance for manufacturing, and rehabilitation of the textile industry, and it provided technical assistance for the development of the metalworking industry.

Turkey also received a series of SALs; these were combined with reform of pricing policies, rationalization of state enterprises, and rehabilitation of credit institutions. In these and other country situations, the Bank and the government agreed on a multiyear program of action that was supported by both SALs and additional sector or project loans.[4]

In several larger countries (e.g., Brazil, China, India, and Mexico), on the other hand, the Bank had made no program or structural adjustment loans up to December 1985. Instead, continued lending for specific sectors or investments has appeared to be the most effective way to proceed.[5]

In the process of helping increase resources for development and improving the efficiency with which they are used, the Bank has often changed both the sector and type of its loan mix. These changes have responded to shifts in country needs, improvement in knowledge, or changes in the external environment. For example, as the consequences of poor nutrition, poor health, and illiteracy became better known in the sixties and seventies, the Bank started to devote more of its loan resources to help overcome these obstacles. And when the "green revolution" opened new vistas of increasing food supplies, the Bank devoted more of its loans to spreading critical know-how among farmers and peasants and helped them with badly needed inputs (i.e., water, fertilizer, and seed).

Now, in the mid-eighties, the restructuring of the economies of several countries calls for more domestic and external finance. The Bank has been assisting these countries in part by accelerating its existing loan disbursements but also by increasing the proportion of its loans addressed to sector or economywide policy change.[6] In 1984 and 1985, about *half* of the World Bank's loans and credits were for purposes other than specific investments; in 1980 these types of loans had made up only about one-third of total lending.

Loan Conditions

All World Bank loans include "conditions" or "understandings." The Bank has given little publicity to its loan conditions although it has discussed its lending experience in detail in different sector policy papers.[7] The conditions are expressed in the loan agreements, which are public documents, but they may be contained in "side letters" or letters of understanding, which are not commonly published. The nature of these conditions varies with the objective of the loan. Essentially they concern project performance, but as the objective of lending has broadened, the conditions are increasingly related to a country's economic policies. They often involve institutions that are important in public investment planning and execution and in the operations of government or specific businesses.

The large extent to which the World Bank's loan conditions have been accepted in practice by individual borrowing countries as well as by creditor governments and institutions is testimony both to the close and productive working relations between the Bank and its borrowers and to the skill with which conditions have been prepared and applied. The Bank must necessarily strike a balance among such diverse factors as expediency, borrowers' attitudes, and the expectations of creditor governments. In general discussions on Bank lending policies, LDC representatives have often sought to limit the Bank's conditions and avoid cross-conditionality with the IMF (see chap. 7). On the other hand, several creditor governments have wanted loan conditions that gave greater emphasis to the adoption by LDCs of more market-oriented policies.

One major objective of the Bank's loan conditions is that its loan funds be well spent. Indeed, as a key operating principle in lending for *specific* investment projects or programs, the Bank never disburses a single dollar, yen, or any other currency without knowing the precise purpose of the expenditure. This is true for each project, however small and specific, and has broad policy implications. It sets a standard for management of the entire public sector, and it helps reduce corrupt or unbusinesslike behavior on individual projects. And while it cannot be said to have eliminated *all* unbusinesslike behavior, it has safeguarded against misuse of Bank project loan funds.

In a broader sense, World Bank loan conditions aim at increasing savings and improving resource allocation—in other words, helping channel expenditures toward purposes from which the country can achieve the greatest benefits. The larger or more strategic the project, the greater the likely impact of the loan conditions on economic management. The Bank's conditions seldom cut into a country's real income level but instead are designed in a longer-term framework to help increase output and investment, and their implementation can often be shared by several sectors of the economy. On the other hand, the Bank's insistence on sound pricing policies and enterprise autonomy can be controversial, and some LDC policymakers may feel it interferes unduly in internal affairs.

The structure and autonomy of the borrowing entity has

long been of central concern to the Bank. While governments must guarantee all World Bank loans, the loan conditions try to place the borrowing entity beyond the reach of political intervention and to assure that the entity can be run in a businesslike manner and without unnecessary reliance on central government finance. This condition was of special importance in the Latin American countries in the fifties and sixties, when they were building their electric utilities, transportation, and industrial enterprises.[8] Many of these countries would have avoided some of the domestic financial dislocations that accompanied the debt crisis if their investment policies in the seventies had adhered to the principles of autonomy and rational pricing envisaged in the Bank's loan conditions for individual borrowing entities. Today this type of condition continues to be essential to all policy reform, especially in Africa, and its relevance underscores the central role that project finance can play everywhere.

Yet, in general, it is probably true that the Bank has suffered from a tendency to attach *too many* conditions to its loans. For example, loans to development banks have often included too many details on institutional development (such as staffing, management, subproject appraisal, and financial criteria), while several SALS have contained too many details on a diversity of sectors (e.g., trade policy, energy, public investment planning). As the Bank begins to focus conditions more sharply and keep them simple, subsequent monitoring and enforcement will also become more feasible.

Condition Specifications

Technical, financial, and economic specifications of loan projects are designed to make them realistic and viable. World Bank projects do not generally suffer from excessive funding, overly optimistic market estimates, or overdesign of capital facilities—faults that unfortunately have often characterized projects financed commercially or with export credits in the 1960s and 1970s. The Bank's insistence on careful preparation and international competitive bidding has saved poor countries hundreds of millions of dollars, the savings often being a significant share of the funds required in "commercial" ventures or bilateral contracts.

Correct pricing is a cornerstone of economic management, and World Bank loan conditions usually seek to ensure that the borrowing entity charges remunerative prices for its products and services, be they electric power, water, fertilizer, or steel; that it similarly pays economic prices for its raw material inputs and other requirements; and that it does not rely on subsidies. Thus, in the fifties and sixties, the Bank maintained a persistent dialogue with Mexico and Colombia—sometimes carried on by the Bank's president (Eugene Black) talking directly to those countries' presidents—against subsidization of public services.

A borrowing entity is also encouraged to produce a sensible return on investment, often a rare phenomenon in the public sector. Such policies on pricing and investment return favorably affect productivity, encourage demand to respond to rational prices, and reduce the financial dependence of the enterprise on the government's budget.

The Bank often attaches "sector" conditions to loans for specific projects and to loans made to finance a phase of a sector agency's investment program (sector investment and maintenance loans). Sector conditions address management and policy issues in an industry or a segment of the economy. For example, a loan for highway construction may contain conditions for the management of highway maintenance or for transportation planning of the country as a whole. Or a loan for a steel plant may contain understandings on the development of the steel industry (as in Brazil). In the seventies, however, as many countries were able to get ample finance from alternative private sources, it became harder for the Bank to "enforce" sector conditions, often to the detriment of investment quality or efficiency.

It must be recognized, moreover, that no single loan or group of loans can overnight eliminate distortions in the level and structure of prices caused by widespread and long-standing government intervention and protection. In some countries, the various forms of government intervention add up to protection exceeding 50 to 100 percent. Such intervention weighs heavily on industrial efficiency and competitiveness as well as on agricultural export activities. Nevertheless, the Bank's attitude on pricing and investment return, if consistently pursued through countrywide programs, can give an important signal to LDC policymakers and other leaders, and support the sound policies now sought by an increasing number of LDCs.

Any condition can, of course, best be applied when it is welcomed by the borrower from the start of the operation. Perhaps the best condition is the one already fulfilled when the loan is signed. It can have a decisive impact in countries, such as many in sub-Saharan Africa, that lack essential institutions and where policy reform is a core issue. It is an art to select those countries and sectors that can be persuaded to adopt policies advocated under Bank loans so that funds can be spent to greatest advantage. In most countries, the ground must be prepared through careful analysis and subsequent dialogue. In those countries (e.g., many of the larger developing countries) that have strong technical proficiency and engage in intensive and systematic internal review, negotiating such conditions becomes a thoroughly collaborative exercise.

Dialogue with Borrowers

The World Bank has always carried on a dialogue with borrowing governments and agencies on many matters of policy, management, and administration. Since 1980 this dialogue has come to include many issues in countrywide policies, although broader discussions were conducted with several countries as early as the fifties and sixties. These discussions have been carried out in a friendly, nonconfrontational spirit, as one would expect from an institution dedicated to close cooperation among member governments. The dialogue places each loan—in fact, the Bank's entire lending strategy—in a broad framework so that better value is obtained from each dollar lent. And as this dialogue is part of the Bank's close working ties with country policymakers and technicians, it should be noted that the word *leverage* does not occur in the Bank's lexicon.

The Bank's discussions are based on staff studies, undertaken in close collaboration with officials of the recipient countries and, where necessary, with the help of expert consultants from the private sector. These studies proceed on three levels, focusing on economywide issues, particular sectors (such as rural development or transportation), and specific investment projects and their executing agencies. Numerous special studies cut across sectors and projects and are concerned with broader policy issues. In practice, there is intense and continuous interchange among all three levels of staff work. No one type of study proceeds without drawing on the other two.[9]

Studies of economywide issues, which the Bank calls "country economic reports," concern policies of efficient allocation of public and private resources, and assess prospects for growth, investment, and balance of payments (including external debt). They analyze questions of finance for long-term investment from all sources, the country's creditworthiness, the appropriate blend of short- and long-term finance, the management of public investment and the role of state enterprises, and the improvement in domestic financial markets and their contributions to the financing of private enterprise. These economic studies, along with sector-specific studies, are basic to the Bank's discussion of development management, the level and terms of long-term finance, and the formulation of an external lending strategy for the country. The issues in the management of the country's development and the contributions the Bank can make to help resolve them should determine the Bank's own lending strategy and the design of individual loans.

In carrying out its dialogue, the Bank has the advantage of working continuously not merely with the central financial authorities, but also with several key operating ministries and agencies responsible for principal development sectors. Hence, its policy advice can be intimately linked with building up the very institutions that must formulate and carry out economic policies—for example, ministries of agriculture, industry, and energy; public utilities; development banks; etc.

The close operational links with institutions and policymakers have enabled the Bank to be of help when countries face difficult problems of change. Mention has already been made of how Bank lending supported policy change in the Philippines (1980–82). In the early seventies, the Bank assisted Brazil in her then successful stabilization efforts and in laying the basis for a better transportation system and for expanded steel production, all essential for subsequent acceleration in growth. For three decades the Bank has collaborated with Colombian officials, business leaders, and economists in determining development priorities, improving financial policies, and mobilizing external capital. Since 1968, through its resident staff, the Bank has helped Indonesia in macroeconomic management and investment planning, and has worked closely with India in improving her agricultural policies and food production, as well as in many other activities, such as development of investment banking, rationalization of basic product pricing, and liberalization of investment and import controls. Finally, in the last few years, the Bank's experience has been a source of information for Chinese officials in their search for a more rational economic policy. In these and many other countries, dialogue on crucial aspects of development contributed to later policy reform; critical policy changes were accompanied by a high and rising level of World Bank lending, matched by the Bank's encouragement to other lenders to help the countries' external capital requirements.

Lastly, the Bank's policy assistance has been essentially a *cooperative* venture with the recipient countries. Successful country programs must be homegrown and cannot be standardized or externally imposed; they should be designed and perceived as central to the countries' own interests. The Bank plays a supplemental role, backing up and helping to implement sound policy initiatives. In so doing, the Bank gives new meaning to Eugene Black's term "development diplomacy." The Bank must continue to build on its record of being present when countries need its help most, of providing useful advice, and of tailoring its lending to the needs of the individual situation.

Sharpening the Bank's Focus on Policy

The changes in the international environment (see chap. 4) have made economic policy reform of even greater interest to developing countries than it was in the previous two decades. Delay can make countries more vulnerable to the greater volatility in trade and finacial flows and can also increase the cost of adjustment. Fiercer international competition makes restructuring of the LDC economies a central issue for them. Consequently, the Bank has greatly increased the proportion of its loans addressed to broader issues of development management. As has been noted, more than half its loans now go for programs that extend beyond specific investments and are concerned with sector or broader economic policies. The Bank's global knowledge of sector developments, its technical capacity, and its links with a variety of key operating agencies enhance its effectiveness in policy assistance. In view of the increased importance of policy-based lending, it it useful to review its consequences for the World Bank's lending policies and management.

Determining both the level and direction of World Bank lending involves policy evaluation and discussion among numerous LDC officials and many and various Bank experts. Broader policy considerations need to be applied to all its lending, including even that for specific projects. But the Bank has yet to clarify comprehensively and concretely what it regards as sound development policy, and how its loan conditions are applied in particular country situations. When a new World Bank president took office in mid-1986, the Bank's standards of policy judgments still had not been formulated explicitly in a general statement subject to review by its executive directors, made clear to its operating staff, and published.

The Bank has understandably found it difficult to issue simple and consistent yet comprehensive guidelines for evaluating development policy.[10] Performance standards, which are continually being adapted to meet changing domestic and international conditions, have changed markedly over the years. In the 1950s and 1960s, mobilization of domestic finance for high-priority investments, and avoidance of both public investments with poor economic returns and excessive external borrowing for inappropriate purposes, received strongly positive marks.[11] In the 1970s, additional emphasis was placed on improving income distribution, human capital, and productivity of the poorer population groups. Studies of price incentives initiated in the 1960s were increasingly applied in the 1970s as the Bank sought to redress the policy bias against agriculture and exports. This emphasis has continued in more recent years as the Bank has stressed the importance of increasing efficiency throughout the economy, inter alia, through restructuring, better balance between the private and public sectors, and recovery of domestic financial markets. The *World Development Report 1986* paid special attention to the importance of agricultural incentives.

Based on the Bank's experience over the years, one would

expect that new operational guidelines would give top ratings to efficient resource use, mobilization of savings, recognition of the essential role of market forces, and decentralization and autonomy within the public sector; careful establishment of priorities for public investment; good economic, financial, and technical "housekeeping" on projects; and reform and recovery of domestic financial markets and of the private sector (or, in Socialist countries, decentralized small- and medium-size industries). Such operational objectives would also make a positive contribution to creation of employment opportunities and to alleviation of widespread poverty through improved productivity and the provision of basic services with a high economic yield.

If World Bank operations are to give more central attention to countries' policy performance, the Bank must be able to keep its lending flexible. The realization of the Bank's own lending targets should not be a standard of its success. Yet the speed and level of Bank loan disbursements may be undeniably critical to the ability of governments to improve policies and management in selected situations. A high and increasing level of Bank lending will be particularly important in the years ahead in countries that have an agreement with the Bank on policies and project performance, and especially in those that require finance in support of new growth-oriented policies. Of course, an increase in lending to individual countries must always allow for the availability of loans from other sources, and it must avoid overconcentration of Bank loans in any single country.

Making Bank lending conditional on adequate policy performance not only improves the quality of the Bank's loan portfolio, since countries meeting high policy standards are also more creditworthy, but also, over the longer term, and as countries with continued favorable performance mobilize sufficient finance from private sources, will permit the Bank to scale back its own lending to them. In fact, the Bank has sought to standardize this process under a "graduation" policy, which requires it to phase out lending over a five-year period to countries above a certain per capita income ($2,850 in 1986). Even in these situation, however, the Bank can argue for continued lending if the country concerned cannot meet the primary needs of a reasonable development program.

In practice, the extent of Bank lending will most likely be determined by actual market conditions, with the Bank lending less as countries become able to attract more private capital. One would also expect that the Bank will maintain a presence as long as its technical contribution and its catalyzing function are in demand (see chap. 7). Some of the higher-income countries no longer in need of Bank loans should, of course, reimburse the Bank for its technical assistance (as, e.g., Saudi Arabia and some Arabian Gulf countries have been doing for some time).

Until 1985 the level of the Bank's structural adjustment lending had been confined by the Bank's own resource anticipation and, technically, by the rule that SALs must stay below 10 percent of lending to individual countries. But lending limits of this kind are necessarily constraining and may impede suitable lending strategies. Thus, since 1984 the Bank has diversified its lending in support of adjustments by linking its loans to adjustments in specific policies (e.g., trade) and in specific sectors, as well as to adjustments in economywide policies. In 1986, total lending in support of adjustment policies was estimated at 15 to 20 percent of total lending and at 30 to 50 percent of lending to some major debtor countries.

Flexibility in Bank lending is reflected both in the varying mix of program, sector, and project lending and in the changes in purpose and design of projects. Overall, program lending need not increase drastically at the expense of specific projects. Of course, a temporarily depressed level of local savings will inhibit lending for specific investments. But programs under SALs address particular policy issues, including increasing savings and exports. Over the longer term, program lending must be supported and followed up by loans for specific projects and sectors, in which the Bank has shown a strong record of performance. The mix of program and project lending is illustrated by the Bank's operations in Turkey, where, besides loans for structural adjustment, the Bank also lent for a wide variety of projects including electric power, highways and ports, irrigation, the pulp and paper industry, industrial training, and urban planning.

But what about the disadvantages of financing specific projects? For example, before joining the Bank staff, Anne Krueger claimed that it is hard to stop disbursements on project loans when a country's policies deteriorate. [12]

In actual practice, however, poor project and policy performance will often slow down disbursement of existing loans. But the Bank's experience has also shown that stopping disbursements abruptly or frequently may harm the execution of sound investments and lead to confrontation, which hardly fits a longer-run relationship of constructive cooperation. By continuing disbursements the Bank is able to maintain a "presence" vis-a-vis many ministries and operating agencies, and this presence can be used quickly when the tide turns and the country needs advice and assistance. Further, the Bank can and often has given crucial signals to policymakers by varying its level of new commitments, a reduction of which can avoid a buildup of loans outstanding to countries with deteriorating policy performance and creditworthiness.

An early example of the impact the Bank can have by stopping negotiation of new loans was the breakdown of Colombia's dictatorship and subsequent restoration of constitutional government in 1956. Deeply concerned with unwise public expenditure policies and excessive foreign borrowing, the Bank undertook an in-depth survey of Colombia's public investments in 1955. But the mission's report was totally ignored by the dictator, Gustavo Rojas Pinilla, who instead proceeded with discussions on an offer of $300 million of supplier credits—a very large sum at the time. In September 1956, faced with continued wasteful policies in Colombia, the Bank notified its borrowers in various parts of the country that it was stopping all consideration of new loans forthwith. The move was welcomed by local government and business leaders, who were aroused by spending mismanagement throughout the country. Within a few months the dictator was dismissed and succeeded by the government of Alberto Lleras Camargo, and the Bank soon resumed loan discussions. The new government undertook realistic economic planning and, with Bank assistance, prepared a new four-year investment program. The financial policies underlying this program formed the basis for the start-up of the Bank's first consultative group (1963), in which the Bank worked closely with the United States and the IMF (see chap. 7).

Another unduly defeatist argument against linking lending to country policies is that the Bank can exert but a limited influence on policies because it finances only a minor fraction of a country's external capital inflow—and, of course, an even smaller percentage of its total capital spending.[13] But this negative assessment is not borne out by actual experience in many country situations where the Bank has had a large and diverse lending program and, at the same time, has worked closely with the country's authorities and other external lenders.

In fact, the impact of the Bank's lending is enhanced by many factors: for example, the technical assistance associated with lending reaches many domestic institutions, policymakers, and technicians, and hence extends well beyond the mere transfer of finance; moreover, most Bank loans are now combined with finance from other sources, both official and private, in concerted efforts such as Consultative Groups and joint or parallel financing (see chap. 7).

None of these arguments denies that fitting a lending program of diverse projects and programs into a coherent whole with a clear policy focus is often difficult and complex. It is therefore important that the Bank's operation be conducted within the framework of *country programs*, which provide a comprehensive strategy for the design and sequencing of individual loans and other operations. Based on country-specific economic and operational analysis, these programs identify both the domestic obstacles to growth, which vary greatly among different countries, and the contributions the Bank (and other lenders) can make to help overcome them. The programs also specify basic issues of creditworthiness and development policy, which must be addressed in discussions with the government and implementation of the loan program. For most countries in which it is an active lender, the Bank since the McNamara presidency has prepared such country programs; but until 1986, they were primarily internal documents and had yet to play a central role in discussions with both recipient countries and other lenders on new long-term external finance.

Consequences for the Bank's Management

Giving country economic policy performance a central place in lending decisions has repercussions for the Bank's senior management, its economic staff, and its Board of Executive Directors. To enhance the Bank's effectiveness, senior management must be directly involved in country policy evaluation and discussions with member countries. In addition, it must speak out on policy criteria from an international perspective. Senior management also has the very complex and difficult task of supervising the formulation and execution of country programs composed of many projects and programs designed to have a clear link to development management and policy. Project lending must not be an "easy option" for countries without adequate policies.[14] Instead, the country's and the Bank's views on development strategy and policy must be translated into the design of projects and carried out in a sequence that will best serve the country's development objectives. The Bank's staff with expertise in development policy must be strengthened and given direct line responsibility for economic operations. And government representatives must be brought into the discussion of country programs. These changes may also make working relations with the IMF easier and more effective (see chap. 7).

Once economic and sector policy work is recognized as a central operational function, the Bank's senior management must, of course, give strong direction to it and assume responsibility for it. This breaks with past Bank practice, which delegates evaluation and negotiation of country policy issues to more junior staff levels or treats economists as "staff" rather than "line" officers. As part of a reorientation of Bank lending policies, country policy work deserves the same operational attention as has heretofore been given to project and program matters. Economic policy issues are already of central concern in preparing and implementing SALs, but SALs and sector adjustment loans make up only part of the Bank's lending. The requirements of policy-focused work are not as yet reflected adequately in the Bank's organization and procedures for *all* lending operations.

The Bank's country programs can be of value to representatives of governments and other international lenders who seek to improve the flow of long-term capital. They can also benefit the Bank's executive directors, who must approve each loan but who now do not normally see the country programs. In general, the Bank's board reviews administrative matters and lending and financial policy, as well as important new initiatives such as the recent proposal for a Multilateral Investment Guarantee Agency. In connection with each loan, the board hears the Bank's assessment of country economic policies and prospects and is asked to approve the loan conditions, which, in the case of SALs and other program-type loans, already include important aspects of the country's policies and development management. As economic policy is brought more and more into the center of lending decisions and strategy, it seems natural, therefore, that the board be given an opportunity to consider the whole of the Bank's program for each individual country. To be sure, such a country review must be encouraged by all member goverments of both industrial and developing countries, and, to make the review meaningful, the executive directors representing the countries should be highly qualified individuals with experience in economic policy.

Although the foregoing suggestions envisage a further evolution of the Bank's function, the Bank had already started to firm up the links between country policies and lending operations under Clausen's presidency. And project lending, development management, and country policies have, in fact, been linked in practice in several country situations as far back as twenty years ago: consider the Bank's operational and economic work in the sixties with several Latin American countries, including Brazil, Mexico, Colombia, Chile, and Peru. In 1964, for example, the Bank sent to Brazil an economic mission of twenty, headed by the author, to undertake a comprehensive assessment of Brazil's economic policies and prospects. Based on the mission's report, the Bank reached an understanding with the Brazilian government on its policies, and President Woods conducted a board meeting on Brazil's economic policies and priorities before the Bank embarked on a major increase in lending.

However, broader policy questions continued to take a back seat in many other lending operations. Moreover, in the seventies, the Bank paid increasing attention to questions of poverty and income distribution, and it deemphasized its advice on overall investment programs and policies. As a result, Bank operations and procedures were never changed sufficiently to make its policy focus both clear and applicable to *all* lending operations.

The changes in World Bank procedures suggested here do not require an increase in staff. For many years the Bank has been expanding its operations at increasing cost; the number of professionals required per operation (i.e., per project completed for commitment) increased from nine in 1965 to twelve in 1985, and overall the staff averaged an annual expansion of 7.2 percent from 1980 to 1985.

Although in the past few years, staff expansion has slowed down to less than 1 percent annually, expenditures on staff and consultants increased to $500 million in FY 1986 (or by 3.9 percent over FY 1985), and in FY 1987 they were budgeted to rise a further 4.8 percent. Thus, few observers would disagree that, after many years of rapid staff expansion, the time has come for keeping staff at a stable level and to focus operations more sharply on policy through redeployment and retraining of *existing* staff. Since the Bank's operations need an improved ability to deliver advice on country economic policies, redeployment may mean an integration of research staff into operations. Streamlining existing functions could make possible significant economies in staff and give staff a keener sense of urgency and efficiency. At the same time, it must be recognized that the Bank's technical and policy assistance, in connection with its lending, is a labor-intensive activity, and since it is at the heart of Bank lending, it is not likely to be reduced in the foerseeable future.

Operations Evaluation

Sharper focus on policy issues not only has implications for the direction of the Bank's many operations, but also will change the nature of the operations evaluation, an area in which the Bank has been a pioneer. For each project the Bank's staff prepares a completion report after the loan is disbursed; the report assesses the extent to which objectives were achieved and expectations at the time of appraisal and negotiations were met. These reports are reviewed by the

Operations Evaluation Staff, whose senior manager, the director-general for Operations Evaluation, reports to the Bank's Board of Executive Directors. The reports are then considered by an audit committee of the executive directors. The Bank publishes the results of the operations evaluation annually; an overview of the first ten annual operations evaluation reports was completed in mid-1984.[15]

This evaluation process sets an example for objective and critical assessment of operational decisions and their implementation. It could be adopted to advantage by other international institutions, by the international departments of commercial banks, and by LDC governments. Moreover, as the Bank's own operations evaluation becomes more important, greater responsibility could be given to highly qualified outside experts.

The great bulk of the Bank's evaluation reports to date concerns vital project detail. The reports show, where possible, the economic rate of return as a summary indicator of a project's merit. The rate of return is reestimated at the time of project completion, but even then it may be subject to error and uncertainty. Most projects have satisfactory rates of return—almost 18 percent per annum on average (weighted by project costs). Attainment of project objectives has also been satisfactory. But there was a trend toward increased failure rates in 1977–82—that is, a growing proportion of projects that did not achieve their main objectives or were still on the way to doing so at the time of audit. This unfavorable trend reflected the risks and innovations the Bank started to undertake in the seventies, particularly in sub-Saharan Africa and in agriculture, the sector where the Bank greatly increased its activities and had to face problems of organization, policy, and new technologies.

The Bank's executive directors and management will want to watch trends in project performance closely in the years immediately ahead. While the Bank can and should be more innovative than commercial lenders, failing projects are poor vehicles for encouraging better policy performance. As the Bank enters a new phase of more policy-focused operations, its own evaluation and appraisal processes should also center attention on the impact of country programs with many different projects on policies throughout the economy. This topic deserves careful review by the executive directors, the results of which will command considerable outside attention and are of crucial interest to the future growth and financing requirements of the World Bank.

7

Working with Other
Sources of Finance

THE WORLD BANK has always maintained close working
relations with other providers of finance. Its Articles of
Agreement consider promotion of private foreign investment
a key purpose of the Bank; the Bank is to "encourage international investment for the development of the productive
resources of members" (Article I (ii) and (iii)). The world
debt crisis and the ensuing scarcity of capital have given
new urgency to the Bank's "catalytic function," through
which it facilitates assistance and finance from other sources.

With its affiliate, the IFC, the Bank works not only with
private banks but also with private direct investors, portfolio investors, buyers and sellers of bonds, insurance companies, etc., as well as with official aid agencies, export credit
agencies, and multilateral development banks. In working
with all these different sources of finance, the Bank keeps
abreast of the many changes that have occurred in financial practices and in the availability of capital. In addition,

the Bank's working relationship with its Bretton Woods twin, the IMF, has become a crucial element in the emerging pattern of international financial cooperation. In 1982–84, the IMF helped initiate and then support programs for overcoming debt servicing difficulties and for adjustment in major debtor countries. Its focus on balance-of-payments adjustment and finance is complemented by the Bank's attention to longer-term development.

The Bank's Catalytic Functions

The Bank is a strange institution in that it must seek to create conditions in which *others* are encouraged to provide financial and technical assistance. It can act as a catalyst in many ways: through the design of its own projects and lending strategy, which make participation more attractive to others; through provision of information about development priorities, prospects, and policies, as well as about suitable projects; through its own advice and assistance to policies that encourage sound development and private investment; and, where appropriate, through direct participation of others in financing Bank project and technical assistance work. Besides its own operations strategy, the instruments that are particularly useful are coordination of external assistance and cofinancing with other lenders.

The Bank's catalytic function is central to the exercise of its current responsibilities, and it will be increasingly so in future years. It has also become more complex, as many more channels of finance and assistance have opened up, more banks and agencies are providing external capital, and the ability of the developing countries to attract and use external capital has become more differentiated. This has implications for its relations with member countries and other lenders. How can the Bank best conduct its own affairs so as to increase the total flow of capital from *all* sources? What is the proper mix of Bank lending and capital flows from other sources?

The many ongoing innovations in international finance have affected relations between the World Bank and private lenders and may also help make development finance more effective and stable. It is important to realize that the different forms of development finance complement each other. The World Bank provides *long-term* finance for investment; thus, its operations aim at strengthening the base for growth and diversification in developing countries and so emphasize the essential link between external finance and the investment process. In its initial response to the 1982 debt crisis, the Bank took a back seat to the IMF, acting mainly through an acceleration of disbursements and an increase in quickly disbursed policy-based lending. For its part, the IMF increased its financial assistance for programs of adjustment and debt restructuring, acting in conjunction mainly with private banks. The commercial banks, which had to participate in debt restructuring in individual countries, improved their own economic intelligence and information about creditworthiness, in part through the new Institute for International Finance. Although this institute provides useful information services to the smaller banks, better information has not persuaded these banks to resume new lending.

Looking ahead, it is in the interest of all parties to ensure that the flow of capital be more stable and less subject to the kind of costly interruptions experienced since 1982. The debt crisis and its aftermath drastically shifted the general policy emphasis from development and growth to stabilization and financial adjustment and, along with other causes, were associated with deep cuts in domestic expenditures in many debtor countries. While interruptions of this kind have occurred before, notably during the 1930s, the present debtor countries and the providers of external capital each have the means to improve their own performance and financial policies and practices, which can aid in the restoration of more adequate and stable capital flows.

The World Bank can contribute to these improvements by helping countries obtain a better mix between short-, medium-, and long-term finance, including, where possible, an *increase* in the maturities for project loans. Steps can also be taken to improve the use of available capital. More can be done to spread the risk of lending for development among different creditors, including establishing secondary markets for LDC liabilities, creating a limited scheme for insuring bank portfolios, and making repayment terms more responsive to fluctuations in foreign exchange earnings of borrowers.[1] These steps, which call for study and experimentation, cannot be expected to produce quick and sweeping results. They require a pragmatic attitude and close collaboration among various participants. But only a willingness to change and innovate can bring about the improvements that experience strongly suggests are needed.

Although the developing countries absorb only a small portion of total international capital flows, it is also in the interest of all concerned that they participate in the various measures needed to improve the level, use, terms, and stability of finance. More effective utilization and coordination of external capital assistance cannot be achieved without full involvement of recipient countries; the latter will be more effective where the recipient countries themselves actually assume the lead. The major debtor countries will also have to be in the vanguard of exercising greater caution in new borrowing, and in promoting export development and more efficient use of resources.

As discussed previously, the Bank, as a membership institution, can enhance participation of policymakers of developing countries, both in decisions on individual country operations and in more general policy discussions. Here the Joint Bank-Fund Development Committee, in which finance ministers of the developing countries play a leading role, has already become a useful forum for discussing improvements in development finance.[2]

The Bank's Coordinating Role

Coordinating the activities of the many providers of capital can help increase the level and effectiveness of external assistance. Compared with its role in the sixties and seventies, coordination is today even more necessary because of the greater scarcity of long-term finance and the larger number of banks and official agencies involved. It is important in all countries that look to a steady and high level of capital inflows, including the major debtor nations and such prominent capital importers as Chin and India, and it is especially urgent in sub-Saharan Africa, where improvements in the level and use of aid are badly needed. Coordination is also of central interest to private banks and could make it easier for them to resume voluntary lending to the major debtor countries.

But present circumstances may make such effective coordination even harder to achieve than in the past. Country economies, investment programs, policy issues, and financing needs have become more complex and diverse. Shorter- and longer-term requirements are more closely intertwined, and both deserve urgent attention although often from different groups of creditors. Providers of long-term finance need to consider a greater diversity of projects, sectors, and objectives. The temptation is great for these lenders to proceed independently on a piecemeal basis even though that may eventually prove harmful.

The Bank has for many years paid considerable attention to the promotion of capital flows through appropriate coordination. It aims at improving the flow of long-term capital, not merely its level but also, and often more important, its purposes and terms. Because, in its coordination activities, the Bank has traditionally focused on the adequacy of the countries' development management, it provides in-depth assessments of the countries' development prospects and policies. Experience suggests that the best basis for coordinating external capital is a cautious policy of the recipient country regarding investment and its financing, with emphasis on longer-term growth, exports, efficient resource use, and reasonable balance in the application of domestic and external financial savings. This is borne out by recent events in several East-Asian and Pacific countries, such as Indonesia, Korea, and Thailand, where it was possible to combine coordination of external capital flows with effective debt management. The experience of these countries differed from that of several Latin American countries in that they gave greater play to the private sector and exercised restraint in public-sector management. Such policies make countries less vulnerable to external fluctuation and improve their ability to overcome the impact of adverse development abroad.

Formal coordination by the World Bank first began in the late fifties. Given the preponderance of official finance at the time, coordination was initially aimed at official agencies. The India Consortium, chaired by the Bank, started in 1958 and was soon followed by a similar arrangement for Pakistan and the consultative groups for Colombia (1963) and other Latin American countries. In 1981 the Bank chaired some twenty active country groups and one for the Caribbean countries.[3] Aid groups also exist for Indonesia and Turkey, and one has been proposed for the Central American countries (under the chairmanship of the Inter-American Development Bank). The United Nations Development Programme sponsors twenty-one groups, mostly for smaller countries.[4] The Bank is now trying to organize more coordinating groups for sub-Saharan African countries. In 1985 it set up a new group for Senegal and was preparing other groups in Guinea, Malawi, and Mauritania.

The coordinating groups chaired by the Bank address themselves to the individual country's economic prospects and policies and to the level and nature of its external finance requirements. The Bank has always regarded these groups as forums for presenting and exchanging useful information, rather than as meetings at which participants are pressured into providing certain levels of capital assistance. The first item on the agenda is typically a statement by the recipient country's delegation leader (often the minister of economy or finance) and a discussion of the Bank's country economic report. This might be followed by consideration of a topic of special current interest, such as the country's agricultural or industrial policies or its efforts to improve health or nutrition. For this purpose the Bank usually prepares a special study; the IMF normally participates as well, and its staff representative gives the Fund's view on the country's policies. The discussion focuses on short- as well as longer-term financial issues and provides an opportunity for the government to respond to questions and concerns that participants may have about the country's plans and policies.

The second principal item on the agenda is consideration of a list of porjects and programs regarded as suitable for the support of long-term finance. This so-called project list, which is usually prepared by the government, with assistance when necessary by World Bank staff, indicates the priority and readiness of projects. Follow-up by a local group of aid agency representatives in the recipient country is usually essential; such a group can hold frequent and regular meetings and can monitor progress in program execution. This group may also hold special meetings to focus on projects in a particular sector; coordination of this nature may be useful where there is a strong interest in a particular sector (e.g., electric power or industry) or where more general countrywide coordination is impractical.

The Bank's oldest consultative group is that for Colombia.[5] The experience with this group is of particular interest in understanding both the conditions that make for successful coordination and the difficulties that may be encountered. In Colombia, diverse political and business groups have traditionally given broad support to the country's development efforts. For many years Colombia has prepared and executed realistic plans, policies, and public-sector investment programs, as well as following macroeconomic policies that have avoided high and persistent inflation and prolonged periods of severe overvaluation of its currency.

This does not mean, however, that all has always been well with Colombian policies and that, for example, Colombia has not had her share of disagreements with the IMF or the World Bank, or given irrational protection to some of her industries.[6]

In recent years Colombia's macroeconomic performance has markedly deteriorated; her public-sector deficit exceeded 7 percent of GDP in 1984. She also suffers from serious unemployment. But since the fifties, her budget deficit and inflation have not been as severe as Brazil's and Mexico's, nor has her government entered manufacturing to the same extent as in these latter countries. Further, on many occasions Colombia has taken decisive steps to adapt her policies to her longer-run development objectives. Thus, despite the recent deterioration in her macroeconomic policies, the Bank and other lenders have been able to maintain an extensive and frank dialogue on policies as well as a significant and diversified lending and technical assistance program.

Over the years, the Bank's operations in Colombia have included many "firsts," often representing a Bank response to indigenous initiative and reflecting creative interaction between borrower and lender. Some of these include the Bank's first general survey mission (1949); privatization of the state-owned steel mill, Paz del Rio; organization of a national network of private development banks; and loans for a revolving fund for agricultural mechanization, municipal waterworks, technical education, national transport coordination, interconnection of electric power stations, and a national nutrition program.

Although the Bank has not tried to hold coordinating meetings on the long-term financing of the major debtor nations, in 1985–86 it conducted some twenty consultative group meetings, mostly for small IDA recipients in Africa and elsewhere. The Bank also had meetings on the Philippines, Ghana, Zaire, and the countries of South Asia (India, Pakistan, Bangladesh, and Sri Lanka).

It is useful to recall that the Bank's original policy was to start—and continue—formal coordination only if the recipient country made an adequate effort itself and there was sufficient interest among external lenders and donors. This policy still seems correct in the changing circumstances of the eighties. Coordination cannot work if the recipient country is not fully committed to development and the external participants do not actively seek it. The coordinating approach that evolved in the sixties is still relevant for sub-Saharan Africa and other countries where official assistance plays an important role.

A new emphasis on long-term growth in resolving the debt crisis was evident in the U.S. government initiative announced in October 1985 (see below). One would expect that in this initiative, Bank-led coordination of long-term finance will play a central role. However, to make this happen the Bank's coordinating arrangements will need to be adapted to new circumstances, especially where official and concessional bilateral assistance is progressively being supplanted by private lending, multilateral loans on conventional terms, and export credits. Some countries where this occurs may want to discontinue the formal coordination arrangements, as Korea did in 1984. But as private banks become increasingly important either as creditors or as actual or potential participants in new finance, their participation in World Bank-sponsored arrangements should be of interest to the banks themselves and to the other (official) lenders as well as to the recipient government. In 1982 Colombia once again started a new trend by chairing a consultative group meeting with both private banks and export credit agencies from sixteen countries in addition to the multilateral institutions. Essential economic and project information was prepared with the assistance of the World Bank, which had chaired all previous group meetings. Colombia's innovation may be feasible for other countries.

Private banks should benefit in several ways from active participation in coordinating groups. Most banks cannot undertake the in-depth assessment of development policies and prospects that largely characterizes the World Bank's economic work. Discussion of economic prospects and investment opportunities in an operational context can help banks anticipate shocks and carry out their responsibility for dealing with market fluctuations with adequate but not excessive caution. The consultative groups may also be instrumental in increasing World Bank cofinancing with both private and official agencies.

As conditions change it would be useful to assess continuously the extent to which coordinating arrangements broaden support for policy improvements, improve aid utilization, and increase the flow of external capital. When well conducted, the coordinating forums may also contribute to a realistic assessment of the adequacy of capital flows to individual countries; such a reassessment must underlie the Bank's own presentation in support of its new general capital increase (see chap. 8).

It will also be useful to consider periodically how the coordinating arrangements can be made more responsive to the needs of the recipient countries. As already noted, these countries must be at the center of the coordinating process. Thus, they must initiate or fully participate in the formulation of conditions and policy undertakings, and in the working out of coordinating arrangements and procedures; further, where possible, they must chair the coordinating meetings. Unless they are fully involved, they will understandably regard the conditions and procedures as hamstringing their freedom and the whole operation as a "ganging up" by the creditors.

The International Monetary Fund

Close and effective working relations between the IMF and the World Bank are essential to a strategy of more vigorous and sustained growth in the developing countries, including a more adequate and stable flow of capital. The focus of Fund policies is the restoration of a viable domestic and external financial position. The IMF keeps contact with its member countries about their foreign exchange and monetary policies and provides balance-of-payments finance from its revolving resources. Its credits must normally be repaid within five years or sooner if countries' external payments positions so permit. Since the early seventies, however, the Fund has increasingly recognized the longer-term nature of member-country adjustment problems. Thus, under the IMF Extended Facility introduced in 1974 and the new Structural Adjustment Facility (SAF) initiated in March 1986, members have up to ten years to repay, and in practice, under its various lending facilities, the IMF has been a net provider of finance to many countries over much longer periods—in some as long as twenty years (e.g., Chile, Egypt, and Sri Lanka).[7]

IMF policy understandings with member countries have important implications for longer-term structural growth. Both the IMF and the World Bank are vitally concerned with assuring for their members the benefits of stable and adequate macroeconomic policies affecting their foreign exchange rates, interest rates, and other prices, as well as their fiscal and financial policies. These are all essential ingredients of long-term development policy and are critical to effective Bank operations. The confluence of concerns for the balance of payments and other macroeconomic policies on the one hand and for development programs on the other is particularly evident in the major debtor countries, especially in Latin America and in Africa. In many countries, a sustainable solution to their balance of payments and external debt problems is inextricably linked to a resumption of growth. Hence, the Bank's advice on investment policies and development priorities and the mobilization of finance for development is an indispensable complement to the activities of the IMF.

The Fund has led the global effort to help counteract the initial effects of the international debt crisis that began in the summer of 1982 with Mexico's difficulties in meeting her debt obligations.

Seeking to keep the debt problem from becoming a systemic crisis,[8] the Fund quickly recognized potential national and international consequences and helped several major debtors adopt adjustment programs, some of which may extend over a period of years. The programs are part of a cooperative international strategy, applied country by country, in which commercial banks, central banks, the Bank for International Settlements, governments, and the World Bank participated. The commercial banks agreed to a rescheduling of debts with long grace periods and stretched-out repayments.[9] One hopes the programs will help produce growth through more adequate and longer-term policies, including more rational investment incentives, mobilization of domestic savings, and export development—policy objectives that figure prominently in World Bank country programs. The IMF has supported these adjustment programs with substantial finance from its own resources: Mexico received SDR (special drawing rights) 3.6 billion, Brazil SDR 5 billion. In total, the Fund committed SDR 34 billion between August 1982 and August 1986 to seventy-seven countries, many of which were experiencing debt servicing difficulties. To help finance this burst of IMF activity, the Fund received additional resources from its members of more than SDR 40 billion in 1983.[10]

However, the profound changes in the international economic environment have increased the overlap in the primary concerns of the World Bank and the IMF. Their shared concerns are evident from their operational responses to the debt crisis and to the 1980–82 recession, as well as from their own analyses and prognostications.

As a result of this overlap, their operating staffs are now collaborating more closely over a widening range of operations. Such collaboration takes many forms, including more frequent and better-organized staff and management consultation on country programs, possible staff secondment and participation in each other's missions, and various mechanisms to improve staff familiarity with the often different style and procedures of the other institution. Further, staffs of the two institutions are to work together in elaborating medium-term adjustment programs to be supported by the Fund's Structural Adjustment Facility, which is expected to commit SDR 2.7 billion in eligible low-income countries.[11]

While for many years the Bank and the Fund have respected their distinct and separate responsibilities, they have also recognized a broad "gray area" of common interest. This area was identified in a 1966 memorandum of agreement as including the structure and functioning of financial institutions, the adequacy of money and capital markets, the generation of domestic savings, and the financial implications of economic development for the internal and external financial situation and external debt. A new understanding in 1970 confirmed the earlier arrangement and also mentioned collaboration on missions and collection of statistical data, all of which are crucial to a World Bank role in viable country programs.[12]

In addition to written agreements, much cooperation resulted from improved relations between Fund and Bank economists and other staff, particularly when the two institutions were still small (and housed close together). But in many respects the Bretton Woods twins have each gone their own way, often concerned with bureaucratic turf. Although they operate a joint library and for over twenty years have published a joint periodical (*Finance and Develop-*

ment), they have never merged their macroeconomic research, as had originally been proposed by the Fund's first research director, Edward M. Bernstein. And each institution prepares separate country economic reports and medium-term projections of the balance of payments of developing countries.

As both institutions have grown in size and complexity, staff interaction and cooperation often require systematic encouragement from the top. Yet, even though relations at the working level are now more intense, Bank operating staff often feel they are not backed up by close rapport at the top. Indeed, the two senior managements do not work in symmetric fashion. Lack of rapport has been caused in part by different policy concerns and experience in the two institutions, by poor organization in the Bank, by the Bank's low-key approach to longer-term debt issues, and by the fact that the Bank's presidents have involved themselves less than the Fund's managing directors in policy discussions with key debtor countries.

Until 1985, interaction between the staffs of the Bank and the Fund was concerned primarily with avoiding conflict. Put more positively, cooperation between the two institutions aimed at ensuring that their policy advice and operations programs on individual countries were consistent and compatible. Looking to the future, one hopes that the present intensification of staff contacts will move from avoiding conflict to what may be called "creative complementarity," and that the collaboration will broaden from individual country operations to joint analysis and proposals on more general topics.

A truly global growth strategy would be greatly facilitated by the Fund and the Bank conducting their separate responsibilities in a single unified operation. With technical resources unavailable elsewhere and total combined financial resources exceeding $200 billion, they can exercise considerable clout.

In country programs sponsored jointly by the two institutions, attention must necessarily shift toward growth; only within that framework will the difficult adjustments countries must undertake be feasible, both politically and economically. Since 1985, resolution of the international debt problems has clearly depended on adoption of a strong growth strategy. Better growth performance is essential in attracting new voluntary finance from private banks.

This shift in emphasis occurs while many countries are unable to draw new resources from the IMF and indeed may be called on to repay the IMF. In 1985 the Fund itself projected that developing countries might have to repay $5.4 billion in 1986 as against total net use of Fund credit of $25 billion in 1982–85.[13] Although it is widely recognized that the IMF should not function as a development finance agency but must retain its character of a revolving fund, it may have to give special consideration to countries experiencing longer-term problems that are unable to meet their repayment ("repurchase") obligations (e.g., Sudan and other low-income countries that are eligible under the SAF). The Fund may also help by monitoring monetary policies in countries where it has no standby agreement for credit assistance. This is envisaged under "enhanced surveillance" in countries that have multiyear debt restructuring agreements but no longer have a standby agreement with the IMF.

With new finance from the IMF projected to decline, countries interested in adopting growth-oriented strategies are bound to seek new longer-term finance from the Bank and other sources. In this process, collaboration between the two institutions is likely to become deeper and broader. In recent years, existence of a Fund-supported program has often been a precondition for a World Bank structural adjustment program. One would expect that existence of a multiyear World Bank country program will similarly become a new factor in working out a stabilization program sponsored by the IMF.

On the other hand, greater cooperation on country programs should improve rather than distract from each institution's exercise of its distinct responsibilities. For example, disbursement of Bank loans is important to the financial programs of member countries, many of which have been worked out with IMF help. But the disbursement pattern is only one determinant in the design of Bank lending, and to make it the crucial one could quickly interfere with the Bank's major objectives: to enhance investment and growth, and to help mobilize long-term finance.

Collaboration on country programs should, of course, be backed up by creative complementarity on more general policy issues. Thus, in their more general analyses, the two institutions can reinforce each other. The Fund's views on structural issues, on the effects of trade policies, and on changes in the "real economy" can benefit from the Bank's operational experience, its work on industrial and agricultural adjustment policies, and its research on trade and investment incentives. The Fund can also benefit from the Bank's operational knowledge of how the public sector works and of what is involved in rationalizing state enterprises and reducing public-sector deficits. Likewise, the Bank's analysis of how economic trends in industrial countries affect developing countries could be strengthened by greater familiarity with the Fund's experience in industrial countries. Among general topics of common interest are the compatibility of stabilization and growth in a medium-term framework, possible measures that may realistically be taken to reduce the interest payments burden on developing countries and reverse the present outward transfer of resources from the debtor countries, and the adverse impact of exchange rate relationships among industrial countries on the external payments position of developing countries. Another joint topic is contingency action on international debt management to counteract the impact of a widespread slowdown in industrial countries. Joint analysis and proposals on such general topics would make country programs more realistic and provide a focus for deliberation in the Joint Bank-Fund Development Committee.

Commercial Banks

Private bank credit to the developing countries increased sharply during 1970–81. The decade of the seventies is of special interest since it includes the recycling of "petrodollars," mainly by private banks, and precedes the cutback in private lending following the 1982 debt crisis. Net long-term credits from private banks increased almost four times in *real* terms during this period; and they increased from 15 percent to 27 percent of total long-term flows to the developing countries.[14]

The spectacular rise in private bank credit occurred in a period of growing capital flows to developing countries from *all* sources. Total long-term flows *doubled in real terms* in 1970–81. Besides commercial banks, major contributors were export credit agencies (doubled in real terms), private direct investors (up 69 percent), and official development assistance (up 72 percent).[15]

The commercial banks were able to channel large financial resources to the middle-income countries, operations that will, of course, influence the kind of financial cooperation necessary in the future. However, they continued lending despite early warnings of excessive external borrowing, warnings contained in World Bank country reports on selected countries, and in some reports of the commercial banks' own economists.[16]

The Bank itself has a mixed record in anticipating the debt servicing difficulties and the commercial banks' response in 1982 -85. Many individual country reports discussed domestic policy weaknesses that caused inefficiencies in resource use and encroached on countries' ability to withstand external shocks. The Bank's *World Development Report 1981* was cautious in assessing the prospective problems of debt servicing, anticipating that banks would have to cut back lending to individual countries because of high exposure. But it did not warn against either overborrowing by several countries or unproductive use of funds borrowed from private banks. Nor did it anticipate the likely consequences of an increase in interest rates and of a simultaneous weakening of export markets. And it judged it "highly probable that borrowers and lenders would adapt to changing conditions without precipitating any general crisis of confidence."

Private bank credit was extended on terms that were often not suitable for sound financing of particular investment projects. Moreover, private banks often lent without taking into account necessary adjustment in the borrowing country, nor did they link their operations with high-priority investments. In fact, ample availability of bank credit often postponed rather than encouraged adjustment and made Bank loans and other financing tied to projects less attractive. In some major borrowing countries, the increased flow of private and export credits weakened efforts by the World Bank to help rationalize investment decisions in important industries.[17] Private bank lending to some countries also facilitated substantial capital flight, and banks appeared ill-equipped to exercise control over such misuse of their loan funds.[18]

The cutback in private bank lending since 1982 has severely reduced the flow of finance to the middle-income developing countries and has placed renewed emphasis on the importance of increased official lending. According to the IMF *World Economic Outlook* (April 1986), private flows to fifteeen heavily indebted countries fell from an average inflow of $45 billion in 1981 and 1982 to less than $1 billion in 1983 and 1984, and became an outflow of $4 billion in 1985; the outflow was projected to continue in 1986 and 1987.[19] Credits from private banks to the major debtor countries have been confined to consolidation and restoration of short-term credit lines and the rescheduling of long-term debts. And while the rescheduling has significantly lightened existing debt burdens, private bank operations currently result in a substantial drain on the resources of major debtors. The net outward transfer associated with private long-term credit for major borrowing countries—that is, after allowing for interest and amortization payments—was estimated by the World Bank at $11 billion in 1984 and $21 billion in 1985.[20]

The U.S. initiative announced by Treasury Secretary Baker in October 1985 envisaged that commercial bank lending to the major debtor countries would turn from a negative to a positive net flow of about $7 billion per year over 1986–88. This increase would be matched by a similar rise in lending by the World Bank and the Inter-American Development Bank (IDB). At the time, the initiative was welcomed by most parties even though the proposed lending figures were considered preliminary. But in 1986, the initial year of the initiative, only the Bank managed to increase its lending. The IDB barely maintained its lending pace while the commercial banks continued to reduce their credit positions in developing countries and maintained a negative net flow.

While the years 1982–85 were very difficult for the debtor countries and their major creditors, they also saw an unusual degree of collaboration among debtor governments, private banks, and official agencies. This kind of collaboration will continue to be necessary in the future as private banks return to more normal operations. The impact of private lending on the stability and growth of the world economy can be strengthened by greater attention by private lenders to signals given by the IMF and the World Bank. It seems essential that private bank credits for general purposes should normally be provided only in the context of financial adjustment programs. In lending for development projects, banks would benefit by operating in the framework of country programs worked out by the World Bank (including cofinancing arrangements). In either case, it is in the interest of both lenders and borrowers for more effective control to be exercised over the use of loan funds—for example, avoidance of overuse of any one instrument (as happened with short-term credits to Brazil in 1981)—by tailoring the extent of general balance-of-payments finance to the terms of financial adjustment programs, and project lending terms to project requirements.

In the immediate future, banks may well continue to be reluctant to resume long-term lending and instead prefer making short-term trade financing loans. Even so, an effective framework for long-term finance will encourage resumption of the voluntary lending that is so important to a new, sustained uptrend in long-term finance. Such resumption, however, will depend on several factors, some relating to the banks themselves—for example, an increase in their capital and a reduction in their relative exposure in the developing countries—and some relating to the attitude of regulatory agencies. It may also benefit from various innovations in lending techniques.[21]

Social and political conditions, as well as economic considerations, indicate that most major debtor countries cannot long sustain an outflow of resources. One hopes, therefore, that the major groups of lenders will seek to achieve a positive resource transfer. In turn, debtor countries will have to continue restructuring their economies. A growth-oriented strategy would strengthen world markets and enable the debtor countries to improve their export performance and creditworthiness and to present many more high-yielding investment opportunities than have recently become available.

In this situation, the Bank's consultative groups and other coordinating mechanisms can provide essential information on policies and projects, and can facilitate a concerted approach by various lenders to deal with the external capital needs of individual countries.[22] Already, in some cases, the Bank has organized special country meetings on specific sectors (e.g., metal manufacturing, education, technical assistance). The Bank may also increase its assistance in improving the external debt management of selected countries, a service it has rendered for many years (as in Mexico during the fifties and sixties). And the information provided by the IMF and the World Bank can help banks and private direct investors gear their operations more explicitly to the development needs of the recipient countries. Such coordination may also help the banks anticipate shocks and overcome the excessive caution ("myopia") they exercised following the 1982 debt crisis.

Cofinancing by the World Bank (and the Inter-American Development Bank and other multilateral development banks) can also have important catalytic effects. Cofinancing is used in combination with both private and official finance. Total cofinancing by the Bank in 1984 and 1985 averaged $4.4 billion, of which half was with official agencies and one-fourth each with commercial banks and export credit agencies. In 1986, cofinancing with Bank lending dropped to $3.5 billion, with the decline of cofinancing by private banks and export credit agencies to $405 million and $579 million, respectively.

In cofinancing transactions, the Bank typically prepares the economic, technical, and financial aspects of the project and tries to have its partners contribute substantially to the financing plan. The partners rely on the Bank to monitor the implementation of the project and, where necessary, take action to ensure satisfactory completion.

The impact of cofinancing on the mobilization of new private credit is not easy to assess and is bound to vary from case to case. Private cofinancing has been small in relation to the capital inflow needed for starting and sustaining a new growth momentum. However, lenders have found cofinancing advantageous in enlisting the Bank's professional development expertise, in ensuring that resources are directed toward well-conceived and well-appraised projects, and in reducing their own lending risk. Borrowers favor it because it provides some assurance that high-priority investments can be financed on the best available terms and because it improves their access to various sources of finance.

To stimulate the interest of private banks in additional cofinancing, the Bank has introduced a new "B-loan" technique, in which it participates in a loan syndication for projects. Its participation may be in one of three forms: financing later maturities, guaranteeing repayment of later maturities, or covering a contingent liability.[23] Borrowers may derive benefits in the form of longer maturities and improved terms in prevailing market conditions. As a result of cofinancing, it may be possible to increase loan amounts, shorten negotiation time, and widen the market for syndications. In finance provided, the extent of participation, and the many sectors covered, the experience so far has been encouraging and suggests a basis for further growth.

If cofinancing is to do more to encourage new and additional private bank lending, the IBRD will have to seek such arrangements with private sources on a much higher proportion of its own lending, well above the 9 percent it achieved on average in 1984 and 1985.[24] As part of this effort one could expect the IBRD to increase its cofinancing, particularly with U.S. commercial banks who until 1985 had refrained from these transactions. More substantial cofinancing could thus become available for large structural or sector adjustment loans, for infrastructure projects, and for credit programs in countries who are engaged in restructuring their economies but who are regarded as not creditworthy or as only marginally creditworthy for new commercial bank lending. The Bank would prepare the project or program and itself finance or guarantee the later maturities, as it did in a 1985 $1.1 billion package for Chile. Although they would have no recourse to the IBRD, commercial banks would provide financing because these types of operations improve the quality of their assets (as compared, for example, with general purpose loans). In later years, the banks would have the option to cancel the IBRD guarantee for later maturities (for which they pay a fee) or sell participations to interested nonbanks.

The World Bank may also help improve the flow of export credits. These credits are one form of official (or officially supported) finance that did not increase after the 1982 debt crisis. Net disbursements from these credits declined from over $13 billion in 1980 and 1981 (or 13 percent of total capital receipts of developing countries) to $7.6 billion (or 8 percent of total receipts) in 1983. Underlying this decline were caution in assessing creditworthiness and lack of demand for export finance. Although in the past, these credits were often motivated by the export interests of the industrial countries, an increase in export credits now would seem feasible and in the interest of both the developed and the developing countries. In a concerted strategy the Bank can play an expanded role in collaborating with both users and providers of export credits. It can help make provision of export credits more consistent with development priorities through information on economic prospects and high-priority projects. And cofinancing between the World Bank and export credit agencies may possibly increase; at present, less than 10 percent of OECD (Organization for Economic Cooperation and Development) long-term export credits to developing countries (i.e., with terms over five years) are used in cofinancing with the World Bank.

Private Investment

The cutback in private bank loans and the budgetary constraints on expanding official finance have caused many observers to call for a more active role of private direct investment (PDI) and portfolio investment in financing development.

Private direct investment has always been highly concentrated in several respects. Most of it originated in the United States, the United Kingdom, Germany, and Japan; it was carried out by a rather small number of large firms and was directed to only a few industries (natural resource development and manufacturing). The most important host countries were upper middle-income developing countries—in particular, Brazil and Mexico, and a few countries in East Asia (Hong Kong, Singapore, Malaysia, and the Philippines).

The flow of PDI was stagnant in real terms during 1970–80, amounting to 18 percent of total capital flows to developing countries in 1970, 11 percent in 1980, and 16 percent in 1981. It averaged $13.4 billion in 1980–83 and, according to U.S. data, turned up in 1984 (PDI from the United States to developing countries averaged $6 billion in 1978 and 1979, turned into an outflow from the LCDs of $2 billion in 1982 and 1983, and became again an inflow of $2 billion in 1984.) The IMF estimates that net direct investment flows to non-oil developing countries were at $9 billion in 1979 and 1980, an average of $12 billion in 1981 and 1982, and $9 billion in 1984.

An obvious case can be made for wider participation by more (and smaller) investing firms, more host countries, and more industries (e.g., agribusiness, basic manufacturing, and transportation) to counteract some of the causes of stagnation in PDI. In the past, private direct investment has been discouraged both by the low real interest rates on bank loans in the seventies and by the reluctance of many host countries to encourage external participation in natural resource development. Multinational companies, it was feared, often circumvented local foreign exchange regulations and tax laws. But an increasing number of countries are now becoming more interested in encouraging private investors. For exqample, India, long a reluctant partner, is seeking participation by foreign investors in export industries and industries using advanced technology. Although new private investment in resource development may continue to be discouraged by stagnation in many markets for basic products, some observers, such as those in the Group of Thirty (a private association set up to analyze and discuss international monetary problems), have assessed the future contribution of private investors with optimism.[25]

Economic and financial policies and the business climate are particularly important in attracting foreign investment. A study undertaken for the IFC shows that specific measures taken to encourage private direct investment have often influenced decisions by foreign companies, even though in the end these measures have often worked against the interest of both the country and the companies.[26] The contributions the Bank and the IFC can make toward strengthening the policy environment for private-sector development were discussed earlier. The World Bank can lend for components of private investment projects, particularly infrastructure, and it can help in diversifying private direct investment into new countries and industries. It can further encourage private investment by having experts from the private sector participate in its project work, as already happens in its energy and industry projects.

The IFC seeks to demonstrate that investment in development can be profitable. This has not been easy in recent years since many of its client firms have suffered badly from an adverse business climate, with ill effects on the quality of the IFC's investment portfolio. Nevertheless, the IFC's *finance* expanded steadily, even through the years of recession 1980–83.[27] Its total investments passed the $1 billion mark in 1979 and exceeded $2.3 billion in June 1986. New commitments during 1981–85 averaged $780 million per year and were $1.156 billion in 1986. The IFC proposes to increase its net investments by 7 percent per year in real terms over the next five years; its five-year program (1985–90), which stresses corporate restructuring, agriculture and agribusiness, and oil and gas exploration, envisages total IFC investments of $4.4 billion in 400 companies, and its operations are projected to attract $15 billion in new outside finance. Sub-Saharan Africa and other poor countries receive high priority. To help finance the expansion, the authorized capital of the IFC has been doubled to $1.3 billion.

In several countries the IFC is advising on the development of domestic capital markets, which are needed to capture the potential of portfolio investment in developing countries. In the seventies a few countries emerged as new markets for portfolio investment (e.g., the organization of equity funds for investment in shares in Brazil, India, Korea, and Mexico). The potential for portfolio investment is large, witness the total capitalization of companies quoted on LDC capital markets of $75 billion in 1983 ($133 billion if Hong Kong and Singapore are included). Developing countries would be well advised to open their own capital markets to foreign investors and treat them the same as they do domestic investors.[28]

The IFC seeks to mobilize new portfolio investment through investment trusts such as the Mexican and Korean funds. In 1986 it helped organize the Emerging Markets Growth Fund. This is run by a private management company, with an initial capitalization of $50 million, of which it supplied $10 million. Its purpose is to invest in securities in developing countries with relatively open and well-regulated security markets.[29]

Since 1983 the IFC has helped increase financing for equity investments through conversion of external debt obligations. By early 1987 it had accomplished debt-equity conversions for some eighteen individual companies and was helping a number of countries set up debt-equity conversion funds able to operate on a large scale (e.g., $100-250 million in Mexico and the Philippines). At the same time, several countries have themselves taken steps to encourage private investment through conversion of external debt into domestic equity. At a discount, either on the principal of the debt canceled or on the exchange rate applied, these transactions may be attractive to investors. In many cases, however, the investments are also subject to restrictions on their purpose or on the repatriation of principal or profit. Some countries—for example, Argentina and the Philippines— require that the investor make additional foreign exchange investments at the official rate of exchange. Mexico has given priority to investments in privatized state enterprises or ex-port and job-creating ventures. The total amounts of debt-equity conversions have been substantial in Chile ($1 billion) and Brazil ($2 billion) in 1983–86,[30] but on the whole they are as yet only a small fraction of the total debt that re-mains outstanding.

The World Bank also sought to improve the environment for direct investment through the establishment of the ICSID (International Center for the Settlement of Investment Disputes) in 1965. The center provides mutually acceptable procedures for settling disputes between foreign investors and their host countries. Its membership has been increas-ing and in 1986 reached ninety-six countries.

Finally, the Bank has also encountered wide acceptance of its proposal for a Multilateral Investment Guarantee Agency (MIGA). In October 1985 the Bank's Board of Governors approved the draft convention establishing MIGA. The agency would have an initial capital of $1 billion, of which a small portion is to be paid in the form of cash contributions. It would be autonomous with some link to the Bank, financed and controlled jointly by the home and host countries of investments, which would thus provide a confidence-building framework for policy coopera-tion between governments and private investors. MIGA would complement national insurance programs rather than compete with them, and it would do so both by providing guarantees and coguarantees for investments against non-commercial risks and by supplementing the activities of the

Bank and the IFC in investment promotion.[31] In the words of a recent Bank staff paper:

> Combining these financing, policy and institutional initiatives, the Bank could become the focus of an international effort to expand direct investment. It would recognize that it is not possible to promote direct investment in all countries and industries. Yet, it would also recognize that beneficial direct investment can make a greater contribution to growth of the developing countries than it has done recently.[32]

8

Financing a Growing World Bank

AS HAS BEEN SHOWN, the many tasks facing the World Bank and the demands of a growing world economy require the Bank's lending to continue to grow at a vigorous pace. The poorest countries, especially those in sub-Saharan Africa, have a continuing need for finance on concessionary terms. Without such lending by IDA and other official agencies, defaults or excessive external debts may multiply, and poverty may increase to levels that are inhuman and dangerous from an international viewpoint. On the other hand, the large Asian countries, especially China and India, are quite able to use substantially increased amounts of external capital effectively, and since IDA and other official agencies can no longer provide much of these funds on concessionary terms, the IBRD, together with other sources, is an appropriate provider of increasing loans to these countries on market-related terms.

The sharp decline in private credit flows since 1982 has

severely affected those countries, mostly in the middle-income range, that had come to rely on the commercial banks for most of their external capital needs. These countries, in transition toward improved growth and a stronger creditworthiness, can be assisted significantly by a step-up in lending by the Bank and other official sources, as well as by the Bank's encouragement of increased private credit and direct investment.

The Case for Increased Lending

Since growth is essential for overcoming present excessive debt burdens, countries need to restructure their economies to become more efficient and expand exports. In addition, in their external obligations, the borrowing countries must attain a better balance between short- and long-term finance, between instruments with fixed and variable interest rates, and between debt and equity. Demand for IBRD finance will increase as countries step up their restructuring efforts and new investments. To provide leadership in this process, the Bank must itself be able to increase its lending.

The scale of World Bank lending in reality will depend on progress toward policy improvements in developing countries and on the willingness of governments to enter into and sustain a dialogue on critical growth-related issues. But the Bank's experience in several countries (see chap. 6) suggests that concrete results in policy-based lending will greatly depend on the Bank's ability to provide substantial finance and to respond flexibly to new policy initiatives. In the past, the Bank has been able to support policy improvements by maintaining a significant operational presence in the countries concerned, which it has done through both a large and diverse lending program and the maintenance of close working relations with country officials and other lenders. Absence or reduction of external support in critical country situations can easily abort or weaken policy reform. Thus, flexible lending policies require a forthright posture by the

Bank, including continued efforts to maintain or increase the speed of loan disbursements and a willingness in suitable situations to make loans that cover a higher proportion of total project costs and exceed the limit that until 1985 was kept at $350 million. Further, the Bank has taken steps to slow its "graduation" policy—that is, the policy of phasing out lending to countries in the higher income range.[1] The policy improvements and restructuring in many of these higher-income countries today require long-term lending support, which at present cannot be obtained from private sources. To make this process work, then, these countries must continue to borrow from the World Bank, albeit on a declining scale.

The World Bank cannot aggressively exercise its catalytic function—enhancing the flow of private lending and investment—if its own lending is severely constrained. Especially in the present period of transition, the Bank must be able to take new initiatives in cofinancing and coordination with other sources of capital. A rising and diversified Bank lending program will strengthen countries' ability to attract private capital and the willingness of private sources to increase their new finance.

Finally, a strong World Bank lending posture is in the interest of a growing world economy. The seventies witnessed substantial progress toward integration of the developing countries in the international economy, particularly in finance. The 1982 debt crisis brought this process to an abrupt halt. Developing countries that cannot now obtain access to long-term markets should be able to borrow long-term from the Bank, which was set up to play an intermediary role between private capital markets and the developing countries. It is now in a strong position to exercise this intermediary function, while at the same time the need for long-term finance is greater than at any time in the Bank's history. Long-term loans will help the developing countries continue their integration in the global economy. At a lower level of long-term finance, however, the developing countries may become more isolated as they encounter repeated debt servicing problems and suffer stagnation in out put, investments, and foreign trade.

The Capital Base of the IBRD

In discussing the financing of the World Bank, it is useful to distinguish between the IBRD and IDA. IDA depends almost entirely on allocations from government budgets, while the IBRD depends on government contributions for only a small fraction of its new funding.

The authorized capital of the IBRD was equivalent to SDR 78.6 billion, or $92.6 billion in June 1986.[2] The amount actually subscribed was $77.5 billion, of which $6.7 billion had been paid in. The balance, $70.8 billion, is "callable"— that is, it is not paid in but is available for backin IBRD bonds and permits an increase in loans outstanding. Each year governments have been paying in only a fraction of their new capital subscriptions; currently this fraction is 7.5 percent.[3]

The principal source of new IBRD funding is the sale of bonds, or rather, the net increase in the Bank's long- and medium-term debt. This provided over 70 percent of net disbursements in 1985 (i.e., gross disbursements of loans of $8.9 billion minus repayments of $3.0 billion). In 1985 and 1986 the IBRD obtained new funding as follows (in $ millions):

	1985	1986
Increase in medium- and long-term debt*	5,096	6,362
Internal cash generation	1,455	1,623
Receipts on account of capital subscriptions*	402	635
Sale of loans	329	251

* Before adjustments for currency appreciation and depreciation

The IBRD's internal cash generation (net of administrative cost) results from the difference in the cost of funds to the IBRD (7.15 percent in the year ending June 1986) and the consequent return on average earning assets (10.1 percent in that period). The main sources are the difference between interest payments on outstanding IBRD borrowings and receipts of interest on its outstanding loans (in 1986 the spread was 0.71 percent) and the return on liquid assets.

The IBRD has been able to earn a high return (10.67 percent in the fiscal year ending June 1986) on the liquid assets ($20.1 billion) that it maintains to meet obligations on undisbursed loans. This liquidity fund enables the World Bank to time its own long-term borrowing judiciously. For example, in case intermediate and longer maturities are not available at rates compatible with the Bank's lending rate, the Bank can draw down its liquidity until the market is stabilized.[4]

The IBRD's capital is basic to its ability to increase its future lending for two reasons:

- The "capital limitation". The IBRD charter specifies that total loans outstanding and disbursed cannot exceed subscribed capital and reserves. This requirement is also referred to as the 1:1 gearing ratio between loan obligations and capital assets. In June 1986 total loans outstanding were $61.1 billion as against subscribed capital and reserves of $82.4 billion.

- The "market limitation". This is more severe than the capital limitation. It becomes operative when the IBRD's own debt comes to exceed the "usable" portion of the IBRD's callable capital, that is, the share of the industrial countries (which themselves have an AAA rating in the capital markets).[5] In the view of the IBRD and its bondholders, the quality of IBRD bonds would suffer were the market limitation to be exceeded. Consequently, the IBRD management has always sought to keep the IBRD debt below the usable portion of the callable capital and to increase the capital when this limit comes in sight.

The IBRD, its stockholders (both the industrial and the developing countries), and its bondholders have a common interest in wanting to maintain the highest quality of IBRD bonds. A lowering of the quality below the present AAA rating would disturb the markets for existing bonds, increase the borrowing cost of the IBRD, and hence also increase the cost of its own loans. The quality of IBRD bonds is influenced by three factors:

• the full coverage of IBRD bonds by the usable portion of IBRD capital and its reserve assets;

• the IBRD's own cautious financial and operating policies; and

• the IBRD "preferred position" in case of debt restructuring by one of its borrowing members. Among industrial countries there has been a tacit understanding that when borrowing countries seek to restructure their official debt (i.e., the debt owed to other governments and official agencies), loans owed to the IBRD will not be affected.

Over the years, the IBRD has sought successive increases in capital so as to stay ahead of the market limitation. From this one may conclude that of the above three factors, the first—availability of capital backing for IBRD bonds—is decisive. In practice, the likelihood of a call on the IBRD capital is remote. In the words of one of its officers:

> The Bank has been unable to envision a chain of events that would trigger a call on the "callable capital." First, management, on recognizing the prospect of a cash requirement extending beyond the time frame of its liquidity position—which amounted to $20 billion in June 1986—would most certainly reduce new lending and, thereby, reduce future calls on its liquidity. Further, given its liquidity position, the long maturity of much

of the Bank's debt, the large and stable cash inflows to the Bank from interest and principal
payments, and its large equity base, the amount
of a call on capital would be but a fraction of total
callable capital.[6]

The IBRD has conducted itself like a conservative financial institution with ample liquidity and reserves and a strong
earnings position. In June 1986, its debt-equity ratio was
5.2:1; its liquid assets were $20 billion; and the return on
its average equity was 13.5 percent (FY 1986). Its lending
policies have been cautious, including in-depth assessment
of its borrowers' creditworthiness and of the economic merits
of its loan projects. And it has never suffered a default on
its loans. For these reasons, the third consideration—its
preferred position in situations of official debt
restructuring—is probably of lesser importance. In practice,
the significance of the IBRD preferred position has been
eroded by many other creditors (e.g., the regional development banks) claiming the same privilege.

The IBRD's cautious operating policies are basic to the
willingness of industrial countries to provide callable capital.
Obviously these countries are themselves anxious to ensure
that there will be no call on the IBRD's capital. If the IBRD
were to increase its lending too rapidly to countries with
marginal or weak creditworthiness, the likelihood of default
on IBRD loans would increase.

The Bank's lending and the strength of its own financial
position must, of course, be assessed in the broader context of policies affecting the health of the global economy
and the developing countries. Besides an adequate flow of
capital to the LDCs, these policies include vigorous trade
expansion, greater stability in exchange rates, and lower interest rates. In such a broader context, increased World Bank
lending and other efforts to improve the growth and policy
performance of debtor countries are in the interest of long-

term creditworthiness and hence *reduce* the risk of default.

Present Constraints

The adequacy of the IBRD's capital must be judged against the likely or desirable growth of its lending. For illustrative purposes, consider the consequences of a 10 percent per annum growth in lending. Depending on the pace of inflation—which currently is anticipated to be much lower than in the past—such lending growth would amount to a year-to-year increase of at least 5 percent in real terms. In actuality, IBRD growth could well exceed such a growth rate: for example, at the April 1986 meeting of the Development Committee, the IBRD projected its lending to increase to $21.5 billion by 1990, implying a growth rate of 17 percent per year.[7]

IBRD lending increased at an average rate of 12 percent per annum during 1975-84, ultimately reaching $11.9 billion. In real terms this amounted to 5.9 percent per year.[8] In the fiscal year ending June 1986, IBRD lending increased to $13.2 billion, after dipping to $11.4 billion in 1985. The 1985 decline in Bank lending was caused by a combination of temporary conditions, mainly the difficulties of mounting new projects in the recessionary environment that prevailed in many borrowing countries.

At a 10 percent growth rate in lending, the IBRD would reach the capital limitation in about five years. Thus, the capital constraint would become acute in the early nineties when loans outstanding and disbursed start exceeding the capital and reserves. Anticipating such a capital constraint, the IBRD has for some time been making the case for a general capital increase (GCI). In practice, the market limitation is even more severe;at a 10 percent lending pace it would become acute by the end of this decade.[9]

Both the capital and the market constraints will be felt sooner if the IBRD accelerates the pace of its loan disbursements, as many observers feel is essential in relieving the plight of major debtor countries. The IBRD's loans outstanding and hence its new capital requirements will increase with accelerating disbursements. Thus, unless a capital increase is in sight, IBRD management would be reluctant to increase quickly disbursing loans.

Rapidly disbursing loans (nonproject loans that can be disbursed in two years as against four to five years for investment-specific (project) loans) made up 20 to 25 percent of total lending in 1984 and close to half of lending to some individual countries. But these percentages were brought down in 1985.

The Bank's disbursement ratio has improved considerably in the past fifteen years: while disbursements were only half of commitments in 1971, they rose to 61 percent in 1983 and 72 percent in 1984. In 1984 disbursements were accelerated under the Special Assistance Program (SAP) approved by the executive directors in the previous February. The Bank estimates that SAP operations in 1984 and 1985 resulted in additional disbursements of $4.5 billion, almost compensating for the decline in regular disbursements caused by the recession.[10]

Without a GCI, the IBRD could sustain a level of lending of about SDR 13 billion (about $15 billion in June 1986 dollars) without exceeding the capital or market limitations. As a matter of policy, however, IBRD management has wished to stay below this level unless it obtains an agreement in principle that IBRD capital will be increased.

But keeping lending below a fixed level of SDR 13 billion will not give the IBRD adequate breathing space or sufficient flexibility to meet its responsibilities as a catalyst for private capital and for policy improvements in developing countries. Moreover, at a fixed level of lending, the Bank would soon start *receiving* net transfers from its member countries; in other words, its total loan disbursements would fall short of its receipts of amortization and interest payments. IBRD lending produced a net transfer to LDCs of $2.6 billion in 1985, but in 1986 the transfer fell to $60 million (as a result of loan cancellations and slow disbursements). Thus, instead of acting as an instrument of intermediation between borrowing members and capital markets, the Bank would become an instrument of dis-intermediation—a radical departure from the principles that have guided its role in the past.

Dealing with the Present Capital Constraints

As the capital constraint on new lending becomes more pressing, IBRD officials and others have explored alternative ways to make better use of existing capital. This may be done in three ways: by increasing the so-called gearing ratio (between its loans and guarantees outstanding and its capital and reserves); by making greater use of its guarantee facility; or by selling a higher proportion of its loan portfolio to private investors. These measures may also help the Bank in cofinancing with other lenders or in exercising its catalytic functions, and they would increase the IBRD's exposure to private market forces as advocated by some conservative critics (see chap. 1).

The IBRD gearing ratio of 1:1 (as required by the charter) is conservative when compared with the 15–20:1 ratio of most large commercial banks. Proposals that it be raised to 2:1 have not, however, met with a favorable response by the United States and other large countries, lest the Bank be unduly weakened. It is also feared that a higher ratio would impair the Bank's own creditworthiness in its bond markets and be a breach of faith toward the holders of the Bank's existing bonds (who purchased those bonds on the assumption of a 1:1 ratio).

But it may still be possible to continue increasing new IBRD lending on its present capital base through innovation derived from the Bank's strong standing as a financial institution. For example, the "Bank's Bank" proposal would set up a subsidiary commercial bank, which would be capitalized at $1 billion with World Bank contributions and possibly with outside funds. It would lend, with a gearing ratio of perhaps 5:1, and its loans would finance the early maturities in cofinancing operations with the IBRD. It could thus also make a welcome contribution to the Bank's catalytic function. This proposal was developed in 1983 and 1984, however, which was a time of uncertainty about the Bank's ability to sell long-term bonds at fixed interest rates. The subsidiary bank was expected to mobilize finance with shorter maturities, for which the IBRD's conventional high-risk protection (i.e., the 1:1 gearing ratio) was not necessary. But by mid-1985 and 1986, the market for long-term IBRD bonds at fixed interest rates had revived, and there was less need to pursue ways of raising shorter-term funds. Moreover, the Bank's Bank proposal was thought to undercut the case for a GCI.

The IBRD may also be able to increase operations on its present capital base by making greater use of its guarantee authority. The founders of the IBRD envisaged that the guarantee authority would be a more important instrument of operations than it turned out to be. From the start, the Bank felt that assistance in formulating and executing projects was essential and could best be rendered through direct lending for specific projects. This argument loses force, however, as other lending institutions strengthen their ability to prepare projects. Moreover, guarantees are subject to the same capital limitation as direct loans: neither can exceed subscribed capital and reserves. Hence, a guarantee reduces the amount of direct loans the IBRD can make so that, unless the IBRD capital base is increased substantially, the benefits of guarantees must be weighed against the advantages of direct lending and associated technical assistance. The IBRD's first guarantee of a loan made by another agency occurred only in 1984 to finance a project that had been initiated with IBRD technical assistance.[11]

The guarantee authority may be of particular interest in

furthering cofinancing with private lenders. It may be useful in already creditworthy countries that want to tap new markets or that are entering the private market for the first time. Commercial banks may be attracted to the Bank's guarantee when they seek coverage for special risks or resume voluntary lending for high-priority projects. The amounts involved in these special situations would be moderate at best, but the Bank may be able to achieve a multiplier effect in encouraging a greater capital inflow for sound investment projects or programs.[12] A special guarantee facility could be created for use in financing long-term restructuring programs. If the programs are of high quality and are closely monitored by the IBRD, the guarantee could be based on a higher gearing ratio. For example, with the ratio at 1:5 and with $20 billion of guarantee authority set aside for this purpose, the IBRD could guarantee $100 billion of new restructuring loans from private sources.[13] Such an operation could fit well into the broader growth-oriented strategy advocated by the U.S. treasury secretary in October 1985.

A third way of getting more mileage out of its capital is for the Bank to reduce its portfolio by selling loans to the market. Critics who want the Bank to place more reliance on market mechanisms have advocated this means of raising resources.[14] In the fifties and sixties, the Bank's sale of loans amounted to a much higher proportion of its capital than in recent years. The feasibility of increasing the sale of loans depends on how risky the market perceives the loans to be and on the level of the loan's interest rate relative to the market rate. In addition, the IBRD itself must weigh the cost and benefits of a loan sale against an alternative sale of bonds. The currency composition of loans and bond issues is important since interest rates vary with the currency market; for example, in 1985 the interest rate on U.S. dollar securities was higher than that on yen securities. Selling old loans with relatively low interest rates could entail (book) losses. Selling loans with low risk could lower the quality of the remaining portfolio. Hence, unless managed carefully, extensive loan sales could reduce the Bank's credit standing or impair its capacity to assume new risks, and thus the potential for selling existing loans may be limited.

In September 1985, the IBRD announced a $300 million pilot program to sell participations in loans made to fifteen countries. This operation was not supposed to entail a loss to the IBRD since losses on some loan sales would be offset by profits on others. By June 1986, when sales of loan participations had reached the $300 million target, they had produced a net profit of $11 million in FY 1986.

The salability of new loans may be enhanced by special design of the loan terms. A shortening of maturities of new loans could influence their salability. It would also increase the turnover of capital by reducing the amount of loans outstanding. As discussed at the end of this chapter, some shortening of maturities may be possible in selected situations.

A New General Capital Increase

The measures the IBRD can take to make better use of its present capital can contribute to the Bank's effectiveness as a catalyst and may marginally increase its own lending capacity. But these measures are not expected to put the Bank in a strong enough position in the late eighties to carry out lending and nonfinancial activities commensurate with its full responsibilities. For this purpose the Bank will need a new GCI, the timing and size of which must be considered in the context of the Bank's lending program.

To provide a rough general framework for discussion, a GCI of at least $40 billion may be needed by the end of this decade. Based on the 1986 level of lending, an increase in IBRD lending of 10 percent per year would bring new commitments to $21.5 billion by 1990 and produce net disbursements of $7–8 billion per year. Rapid growth of

IBRD lending is particularly important if private lending continues to stagnate. A faster growth of IBRD lending (i.e., above commitments of $21.5 billion in 1990) would place the necessary capital increase well beyond $40 billion. As discussed later, the GCI would also exceed this amount if the Bank were to relax its lending terms even if only in selected situations.

The capital increase must be considered in the context of realistic estimates of IBRD lending and capital inflows into the major borrowing countries. These in turn can be based on the execution and performance of IBRD-sponsored country programs. Thus, through operational review of such programs, IBRD executive directors, government representatives, and members of consultative groups for individual countries can be brought into a systematic process of preparing the basis for a GCI and keeping the adequacy of the IBRD's capital under review.

Given the importance of a GCI, the objections against continued growth in IBRD operations deserve careful consideration. To start out, it has been argued that a GCI requires a large expenditure of public funds. But in reality the cash cost of a capital increase to government budgets is small or zero. The IBRD has grown into a strong financial institution that can maintain a high level of operation without recourse to new government budget contributions. What it essentially needs is an increase in callable capital. This increase in callable capital represents a contingent liability but requires no cash contributions. And there is every reason to expect that the IBRD will continue its cautious operating and financial policies and hence sustain its excellent record of not having any defaults on its loans and not having to make any calls on its capital.

Another key objection to a GCI is that continued increase in IBRD lending may impair the quality of IBRD loans. While this objection stems from a genuine concern, one would expect that a 10 percent growth rate in Bank lending is compatible with—and indeed essential to—strong development performance in borrowing countries. As already mentioned, the Bank's operations evaluation has identified an upward trend in the failure rate of Bank projects in recent years. But although the risk of this rate increasing exists in the present recessionary environment in many LDCs, this does not mean that the Bank should not cautiously support policies designed to counteract the consequences of slow growth or stagnation in developing countries. The IBRD can increase its operations where governments and other borrowers in the recipient countries can use financial resources effectively; thus, one would expect IBRD lending to expand only to countries that have sound policy performance and can demonstrate that additional external funds will be well used. Without effective IBRD attention to policy performance and development management, the case for a GCI is weak. On the other hand, a stronger link between IBRD lending and country policy considerations will itself require an increasing and more flexible IBRD lending program.

A related concern is the risk of overexposure in major borrowing countries. IBRD management has guarded exposure in individual countries by limiting the country share in the total loans outstanding and the IBRD share in the country's debt service. The country share has normally been kept below 10 percent although this limit has been applied flexibly (i.e., it has been exceeded) when there is a temporary hump or a speed-up in disbursements. The IBRD share in debt service is particularly important in countries such as Colombia or Yugoslavia, which have relied heavily on borrowing from the IBRD.

As the IBRD concentrates on countries with good performance, its portfolio may come to suffer from excessive concentration on a limited number of countries. But it becomes harder to avoid overexposure in individual countries when total IBRD lending stagnates. If such lending does

not increase sufficiently, the IBRD may have to hold back
its operations in countries such as Brazil, Colombia, India,
Mexico, or Yugoslavia, which have been important borrowers in the past. By being able to increase its *total* lending, the Bank is better able to spread risks over a wider
number of countries and avoid excessive concentration in
any one of them.

A further objection is that rising Bank lending would more
easily displace private capital flows to the developing countries and be inconsistent with the Bank's operational emphasis on encouraging private lending and investment.
However, as already discussed, the IBRD must be flexible
in both the level and design of its lending if it is to succeed
as a catalyst in enhancing private lending. Review of IBRD
country programs could also consider how the IBRD may
best conduct its operations vis-a-vis private lenders and investors in individual countries. Effective collaboration of this
kind may help increase private capital flows and dispel fears
that heightened IBRD operations would displace private
lending in the years ahead.

Finally, the question is raised whether growth in IBRD
lending can be prudently financed, even assuming that sufficient callable capital is raised. This legitimate concern has
also been raised on earlier occasions when the growth of
the IBRD was under consideration. The objection has been
proven wrong essentially because of the very size of the
capital markets, the wide diversification of the sales of IBRD
bonds, and the quality of the IBRD loan portfolio. About
one-fourth to one-third of new IBRD bonds are bought by
governments and central banks, and the rest are bought
by private investors. Total bond sales were about $10 billion
in 1984, of which $7 billion was net (of maturing bonds);
in 1985 the IBRD sold $10.4 billion in medium- and long-
term bonds and increased its short-term borrowing by $709
million. Bond sales may increase somewhat in coming years.

The IBRD carries out its bond sales in close consultation

with the national authorities and manages them carefully so as not to upset individual markets; because of its strong liquidity position, it can delay sales when markets are not sufficiently stable. Further, it spreads bond sales over many markets and currencies—thirteen currencies in 1984 and fourteen in 1985. Less than a quarter of its 1984 and 1985 bonds were denominated in U.S. dollars and a substantial portion of them were placed outside the United States. In some years—for example, 1978 and 1979— sales in the United States were an even smaller proportion. Thus, the IBRD has managed to direct its bond sales to those markets where investor demand is strongest and interest rates are most favorable. In short, IBRD bond sales are managed prudently and carried out in the interest of all parties concerned.

The International Development Association

The International Development Association (IDA) lends all its resources to countries with per capita incomes below $730. In fact, most IDA credits (91 percent in 1983–84) go to the poorest countries, those with per capita incomes below $400. These are countries with the most urgent needs: they suffered badly from the 1980–82 recession and are highly vulnerable to external fluctuations because of their dependence on primary commodities. Deterioration in economic performance has been most serious in sub-Saharan Africa.

The poorest countries, except for China and India, have weak creditworthiness for loans on market terms and should only borrow from the IBRD and commercial banks in exceptional circumstances. They cannot yet generate sufficient growth of output and exports to support substantial borrowing on market terms. Even with considerable effort, their own savings fall well below the sizable investments they must make in infrastructure and basic services. They need substantial and *rising* external assistance to overcome their present stagnation and attain a new development momentum. But this assistance must be provided on concessionary terms if the countries are to avoid default.

IDA has been the most important single source of low-interest loans to poor countries; its commitments are about 29 percent of all concessionary finance in low-income Africa and 43 percent in India.[15] These high percentages reflect IDA's rapid growth in the past decade. In the seventies IDA commitments increased more rapidly than total concessional finance, growing by 11 percent in real terms as against 4 percent for all concessionary finance from countries that are members of the OECD Development Assistance Committee (DAC). But despite this rapid growth, IDA has remained smaller than originally envisaged. Although some of its founders mistakenly thought it would eventually overtake the IBRD, IDA commitments were just 30 percent of the IBRD's in 1984. But because of its slow repayment and low interest charges, its transfers (disbursements net of amortization and interest receipts) compare favorably with those of the IBRD. In 1983–85, IDA transfers averaged $2.3 billion as compared with $2.6 billion for the IBRD; in 1986 IDA transfers were $2.8 billion as against only $60 million for the IBRD.

Replenishing IDA Resources

IDA resources come almost entirely from donor government funds, normally provided in replenishments every three years. In 1984, only about $400 million came from other sources, namely repayments of outstanding IDA credits and the transfer of part of IBRD profits. Since IDA has no capital of its own, its operations would be confined to the reflux of outstanding credits if it were to receive no new replenishment funds.

From 1969 until 1981, successive replenishments increased with leaps of 50 percent or more in current dollars; then the sixth replenishment began.[16] IDA-6 (for 1981–83) was originally agreed to be $12 billion, which, if accomplished in three years, would have constituted a significant jump over IDA-5 (1978–80): an increase of 56 percent in current dollars and 29 percent in constant dollars. But actual contributions by the United States were stretched out over a longer period, and IDA commitments had to be held at a stable level in current dollars, even after including special contributions by donors other than the United States. After peaking at $3.8 billion in 1980, IDA commitments averaged $3.3 billion per year during 1981–84. In 1984 they were $3.6 billion, including $400 million in special (non–U.S.) donor contributions to help make up for shortfalls in IDA funds proper. Throughout 1978–84, IDA commitments increased by 18 percent in current dollars, only half the pace of inflation.[17] In 1985 IDA commitments fell back to $3.0 billion.

For the latest replenishment, IDA-7, which was delayed to take effect in July 1985, World Bank management first proposed $16 billion for three years. This would be more than $5 billion per year, or more than 50 percent over recent levels. The Bank's case was based on the urgent plight of the poorest countries (see chap. 5). Further, the Bank argued that China's needs required a substantial further increase in total IDA resources. India and China together have 450 million "absolute poor"—people living below the most minimal standards—compared with 330 million in Africa. And both countries have per capita incomes below $300—well below the critical level of $400 per capita for countries where IDA seeks to concentrate its commitments.

World Bank management spent much energy in pressing for a substantial increase in IDA-7. During IDA-7 replenishment negotiations, Japan, France, and the United Kingdom initially supported a three-year commitment of $14 billion. The European Community subsequently indicated support for a $12 billion replenishment, or $4 billion a year. However, the United States did not want its annual contribution to exceed $750 million, or $2.25 billion for three years, and the other donors did not want the U.S. share to fall below 25 percent. Thus, the IDA-7 replenishment was agreed at $9 billion, permitting IDA to continue at $3 billion per year.

IDA-8, expected to extend over three years starting July 1987, would be increased to $12 billion (or $4 billion per year) under a tentative agreement reached among donor government representatives in September 1986. Thus, the concessionary loans administered by the World Bank would continue at about the same level, measured in real terms, as maintained during the previous three years. This comparison includes the funds from the Special Facility for Sub-Saharan Africa committed for the three years ending July 1987 (see below).

Over the years the shares of individual donors in total IDA resources have reflected the relative economic strength of the donor countries. Since the start of IDA, the United States has contributed 31 percent of IDA cumulative resources. In IDA-5 (1978–80) the U.S. share was 31 percent, in IDA-6 (1981–83) it fell to 27 percent, and in IDA-7 it was 25 percent. Following the United States, the largest contributors today in IDA-7 are Japan (19 percent), Germany (11.5 percent), and the United Kingdom (6.7 percent).[18]

The difficulties of getting agreement in the donor community about the level of IDA replenishment reflect the different views about what IDA-type assistance can achieve in reality and how long it is needed. The questions raised are now more pressing than before because of both the interest of the United States (as well as of other donors) to reduce civilian and, in particular, "welfare" expenditures and the general concern among donor countries to contain budget deficits. This last concern, however, is probably more psychological than economic because contributions to IDA are but a fraction of the donor countries' total budget expenditures although, of course, they represent a higher percentage of budget deficits.

Allocating IDA Resources

Unless total IDA resources are substantially increased, they will necessarily have to be devoted mainly to sub-Saharan Africa, Bangladesh, and a few other countries that face deep-seated difficulties. The case of many sub-Saharan African countries is especially acute since their per capita income has declined or remained stagnant during a period in which aid has continued at a high level.

Fundamentally, poverty is caused by a combination of poor natural resources, poor human conditions, and poor policies. When natural resources are scarce or ill developed, policies are especially important if a country is to attain some momentum of development. The difficult issue is whether IDA can be effective in helping improve policies under the type of conditions that now prevail in most IDA customers. On this question the evidence is fragmentary, and experience needs to be analyzed in greater depth than has been possible so far. To do so would be especially important in making a case for IDA at its present or higher level of operations.

Achieving a vigorous development momentum will be a slow process in many of the present recipients of IDA credits. In addition, the record suggests that much external assistance to sub-Saharan Africa has not been effective. In the World Bank's own judgment—now shared by most donor governments—substantial external capital in sub-Saharan Africa has been wasted for a complexity of reasons, such as excessive emphasis on prestige projects that cannot be justified economically; neglect of expenditures for maintenance, rehabilitation, and current development operations (e.g., training and agricultural extension); and insufficient support from domestic policies.[19] The Bank's own completed projects show a higher rate of failure in Africa than elsewhere, and this rate could well continue high in the future. To improve the effectiveness of external aid, then, IDA is concentrating a growing proportion of its resources in Africa on program-type assistance with a policy focus and is urging other agencies to do likewise. The new Africa facility, administered by IDA and aimed at rapidly disbursing credits in support of policy reform, had donor contributions of $1.2 billion when it began operating in July 1985. These resources grew in FY 1986 to $1.6 billion, enabling the facility to make commitments of $782 million to fifteen countries.

The new emphasis on policy reform is highly appropriate. One would expect that, besides program lending, assistance for more narrowly defined purposes will continue to be crucial. Project-specific assistance is needed to support domestic institutions, which in many African countries are at the core of strengthening development management. Because basic improvements are likely to be slow in coming, use of IDA funds may well turn out to be slow also. This reasoning assumes that IDA will continue to assist specific long-term development projects and programs rather than become a vehicle for short-term balance-of-payments assistance.

Such a cautious and sober judgment is borne out by experience in other countries where IDA has been active. The impact of program lending on policies and the basic conditions that make for better productivity have been moderate at best and have often required many years of IDA assistance. For example, the industrial import program credits to India were stretched over twelve years (1964–76), and in the Bank's own judgment, their results in terms of policy improvements came slowly and were diffuse.[20] Yet the conditions in India at the time were more propitious for development than are those in many African countries today.

Bangladesh's experience may be more relevant in gauging the likely effectiveness of IDA and IDA-type operations

in sub-Saharan Africa. Bangladesh received ten IDA program credits (exceeding $700 million) in 1972–82, the period
following its independence in 1971. In these years Bangladesh
encountered economic, social, and political difficulties comparable to those now faced by some African countries. Many
of the IDA program credits, well designed and supervised,
were directed toward the rehabilitation (and privatization)
of key industries (textiles, jute, and pulp and paper) that
had fallen under the state's domain. The Bank judged the
effectiveness of these credits to be moderate, if not poor,
in terms of output growth, policies, and improved operating
efficiency in the recipient industries.[21] Progress in many
sub-Saharan African countries may not be any faster and
could be slower.

The slow progress in Bangladesh and sub-Saharan Africa
may reflect a fundamentally more difficult situation than
IDA faced elsewhere in its earlier years. Many countries that
were initial IDA recipients needed concessionary assistance
for only a short time and have long since "graduated" to
become borrowers of the IBRD or commercial banks. It is
hard to believe that only fourteen years ago Korea was still
an IDA client. The long list of IDA graduates shows that
most countries need IDA for only a limited period.[22] The
same process of graduation may now be under way in China
and India, countries that now receive a declining share of
IDA resources. But in these countries progress toward creditworthiness for borrowing on IBRD or market terms could
be uncertain and interrupted by the economic consequences
of still widespread poverty.

India may now be in an increasingly stronger position than
ever before to borrow from the IBRD or private banks.
Nevertheless, her government is wise in limiting its borrowing from commercial sources since too rapid a buildup
of commercial debt could precipitate a major crisis of debt
servicing in case India's external environment deteriorates.
In the seventies India received 40 percent of IDA alloca-

tions; her share declined to 30 percent in 1983 and 1984, and to 22 percent in 1985. In total, she has received $13.2 billion, or 36 percent of all IDA commitments through 1985. In FY 1986 India received $625 million in new IDA credits, making her again IDA's largest customer. IDA has been clearly associated with India's progress, notably her self-sufficiency in food, her improved record in output and export growth, and, more recently, her liberalization of internal controls on prices and investment.

But India's development tasks are still formidable, especially eradicating illiteracy, improving health and infrastructure facilities, and furthering development of major river basins. The government is now taking definite steps to liberalize the economy and strengthen private investment. India's private sector can play a much larger role than it has so far, and the economy can benefit considerably from further decontrol. India can relay on more private capital, although the pace of her commercial borrowing should should be constrained by her export growth.

China's ability to turn to commercial markets is also constrained by many factors. Although her recent export and growth performance are a strong plus, she entered the present transition toward wider decentralized decisionmaking and economic incentives at a time when she received virtually no aid whatsoever and interest rates were high. She has made considerable progress in health and other basic needs, but she still suffers from widespread poverty in some regions, is dependent on food imports, and needs far-reaching modernization of her industrial plant and educational facilities. Given her present poverty and the risks inherent in her policy of liberalization, she is by any standard still a logical claimant on IDA. By mid-1985 IDA had extended $1.176 billion to China—less than 9 percent of the total India had received. In FY 1986 China received only $405 million in IDA credits. However, in addition to IDA support, China can effectively use assistance from both private and official finance in laying the base for a larger inflow of long-term capital. As in the case of India, fulfilling China's substantial and varied sector needs will itself be of major benefit to a growing world economy.

Few will deny that at its present level of operations IDA faces a difficult task of rationing and reallocating its resources. India in particular may have to do with a lower share than in recent years, and China had originally expected higher allocations than are now possible. Sub-Saharan Africa will have to receive a larger share, assuming it can improve its use of external capital; in 1982–85 it already obtained more than one-third of IDA commitments.

The case for IDA replenishment will be strengthened by close monitoring of the effectiveness of IDA and IDA-type credits, of the availability of alternative finance, and of the limits of creditworthiness in both small and large countries, but particularly in China and India. Like the IBRD lending program and the case for a general capital increase, IDA replenishment must be considered within a general framework substantiated by the performance of individual country programs. IDA's task is complicated by the presence of many small countries on its roster of recipients. But IDA is already preparing and monitoring programs for the increasing number of countries with a consultative group. One would hope that the process of monitoring individual country programs will be integrated with—and will strengthen—the demonstrated need for IDA replenishment within the donor community. Only in this way can the level of IDA operations be justified convincingly and be put on a firmer, more regular footing.

The Terms of World Bank Lending

There is a steady interplay in the lending operations of IDA and the IBRD. IDA deals with a changing roster of borrowers. As some countries are able to get by with fewer

IDA credits, they will seek to borrow more from the IBRD. The IBRD lends to countries with widely differing levels of income and creditworthiness. And within individual countries the latter is subject to rapid change. Given the many changes now occurring in the categories of borrowing member countries, it would seem a good time to consider the adequacy of the terms on which IDA and IBRD credits are made available to different groups of countries.

Since its inception, IDA has maintained the same terms for its credits: repayment over fifty years with an initial grace period of ten years, during which no amortization takes place; a "service charge" of 0.75 percent on the disbursed balance outstanding on the credit; and, since 1982, a 0.5 percent charge on the undisbursed balance. The interest cost of IDA credits is now much lower than in the past in relation to the interest rates on IBRD or commercial bank loans. The interest rate on IBRD loans moves with those prevailing in the market, which are now much higher than in the sixties, whereas IDA charges have stayed the same. In technical terms, the "grant element' of IDA credits has risen considerably, from 72 percent in the sixties to over 90 percent in recent years.[23]

In September 1986 the Bank announced that the IDA donor governments had tentatively agreed to shorten repayment terms for IDA-8 credits. The maturities of these credits would be reduced from fifty years to forty years for the least developed countries, and to thirty-five years for the other recipients. However, the ten-year grace period would remain unchanged and no interest would be charged (the service charge would remain at 0.75 percent).

There may also be a case for reconsidering the terms of IBRD loans. Apart from the policy or project conditions of these loans, their terms are influenced by the interest cost, the currency mix of the repayment obligation, and the length and scheduling of repayment.

Since the IBRD gets the greater part of its new funds by

borrowing at the going interest rates in capital markets, it disburses its loans in the different currencies it borrows, and it periodically adjusts the interest cost of its loans to keep them in line with changes in the capital market. While IBRD loans are denominated in U.S. dollars, the borrower's obligation is in a currency mix. To even out the currency risk borne by the borrower, the IBRD since 1980 has based the repayment obligation on an actual pool of currencies used in disbursement but not yet repaid at any given time. The interest costs on IBRD loans are determined every six months on a weighted average of all IBRD borrowing outstanding plus a 0.5 percent spread; in the first half of 1986 this amounted to 8.5 percent. Since the interest rate is the average for *all* IBRD borrowing outstanding ($35 billion in the first half of 1986), the actual interest rate on IBRD loans tends to be less volatile than rates in money markets, for example, LIBOR, the interest rate in the London money market, on which commercial loans are frequently based. In addition, IBRD loans carry a 0.5 percent commitment fee on the undisbursed loan balance.[24] The repayment period for IBRD loans is fifteen to twenty years, the period being shorter for countries with greater economic strength (usually as measured by per capita income); repayment actually begins after a three- to six-year grace period, depending on the nature of the project being financed.

The maturity and grace periods of IBRD loans vary with the per capita income of the borrowing country. Thus, in mid-1986 the repayment period varied as follows:

	Per Capita Income of Borrowing Country (in 1984 U.S. dollars)		
	Below $790	Between $790 and $1635	Above $1635
Maturity (yrs)	20	17	15
Grace (yrs) on amortization	5	4	3

Prior to 1977, the IBRD used a mortgage-type repayment schedule (with an even flow of amortization and interest payments), in which repayment of principal was lower in the early years. Since then, the repayment schedule for IBRD loans has been based on an even flow of amortization payments.

Liberalization of IBRD loan terms could consist of a marginal or selective lowering of interest rates. In addition, the IBRD could revert to a mortgage-type service schedule; this would again reduce the outflow of repayments in the early years (in effect increasing the average life of the loan). From the viewpoint of the IBRD, this would increase both the amount of loans outstanding and the capital required to sustain a given pace of commitments. Moreover, liberalization could be applied selectively—for example, by applying a mortgage-type schedule to countries with per capita incomes below $790, while countries with per capita incomes above $790 might obtain longer grace periods (e.g., five years instead of three or four years). The liberalization could also be confined to countries with a sound structural adjustment program monitored by the IBRD.

One may question the justification and practicality of even a selective policy of liberalizing IBRD lending terms. It would be difficult to administer. In addition, such a policy makes sense only if other lenders also liberalize their terms so that concerted action has a significant impact on the borrowing country's program execution. In an enlarged role of dealing with the debt crisis, as envisaged in the Baker initiative, the World Bank would be expected to act in close harmony with other lenders. In any case, acting alone, the IBRD may not have sufficient impact on the debtor country's viability to warrant a softening of lending terms.

Some consideration may also be given to an intermediate, slightly subsidized interest charge on IBRD loans made to the poorer "blend" countries with firm structural adjustment programs. Although IBRD interest charges on all other loans should remain, as at present, in line with market rates, the subsidization of interest rates to some blend countries could be financed from the IBRD's profits or from a marginal increase in the IBRD main lending rate. One would not want to increase the main loan charge too much because this might unduly affect the IBRD's competitiveness vis-a-vis other lenders. (Of course, the IBRD's position in international lending is also influenced by the efficiency with which it provides nonfinancial services, especially technical and policy assistance.) However, a marginal increase in the main loan charge may help sales of new loans to private investors.

Finally, the amortization period for some loans perhaps could be related more directly to the repayment capacity of the project. Self-liquidating projects, such as mining or manufacturing for export, generate their own foreign exchange earnings available for the repayment of the loans. These types of projects can often repay loans more quickly than other types. Shorter repayment periods may thus be justified for selected projects in the relatively richer borrowing countries with stronger creditworthiness. The length of the repayment schedule may be a factor in working out cofinancing arrangements and may influence the salability of the loan to private investors.

9

The Politics
Of the World Bank

TO PLAY A BROADER, more active role in the world
economy, the World Bank needs the strong support of its
member governments. And the evidence seems clear that
these governments, in both industrial and developing countries, have a clear national interest in providing such support, since their international economic objectives are in
many ways backed and enhanced by World Bank operations. While precise objectives vary from country to country, Bank members share many common goals:

• to strengthen financial and economic ties between
developed and developing countries;

• to renew the growth momentum in all LDCs and, particularly in the poorest countries, to strengthen the productive base for overcoming hunger, disease, and other human
suffering, with obvious longer-run beneficial effects on the
well-being and social stability of many regions;

• to sustain policies aimed at a growing, more integrated
world economy, a widening of markets, and increasing trade;
and

- to stimulate an increase in private capital flows to the LDCs and more effective cooperation between official and private sources of capital.

Despite such common objectives, the Bank has not always enjoyed the full measure of support that it deserves in either developing or industrial countries. Even though much of the criticism of the Bank is not founded on actual experience, as earlier chapters have made clear, there are other factors that have impeded full support, particularly in the United States which is still the most important shareholder in the IBRD and provider of IDA funds. (Its share, however has declined over the years as other countries have increased their output and savings; at present the U.S. share in new contributions to IDA is 25 percent and in IBRD capital, about 20 percent. As of June 1986, the U.S. portion of subscribed IBRD capital was 20.9 percent and of paid-in sub-srciptions, 21.6 percent.)

Some critics in the United States and elsewhere doubt that governments can control the allocation of funds contributed to multilateral institutions. In Bauer's words, "Multilateral aid reduces parliamentary control and severs the last vestige between recipient governments and donor taxpayers and their representatives."[1] The best answer to this allegation is that the nonpolitical character of the World Bank, envisaged in its charter, is a strength, not a weakness. This characteristic facilitates a cost-effective and efficient mobilization and allocation of resources. Moreover, Bank lending seldom runs contrary to specific bilateral interests. Over the years, shifts in the orientation of bilateral aid policies have been reflected in changes in Bank operations, and vice versa. Such changes were evident during the Alliance for Progress in the sixties; in the emphasis on participation of the poor in the U.S. "New Directions" aid legislation in the seventies; and in the increased stress on the private-sector role in the eighties.

Some outside critics have a rather simplistic view of how

governments can exert influence on multilateral organizations. In fact, many channels exist for exercising such influence. LDCs can have a significant impact through negotiation on individual loans and on Bank country lending strategy. Both LDCs and industrial countries have representation on the Executive Board and can conduct direct discussions with Bank management. Moreover, industrial countries can express their views during IDA replenishment discussions, in negotiations about IBRD capital and access of the World Bank to their security markets, and in consultative group meetings.

Against the negative judgment of some critics, the U.S. administration has supported the Bank while also calling for a stronger Bank response to the changes in the international environment. In the 1983, 1984, and 1986 annual meetings of the World Bank and the IMF held in Washington, President Reagan, in his opening addresses, spoke favorably of both Bretton Woods institutions. In its 1982 report on U.S. participation, the Treasury Department recommended that the United States continue to play a major role in the World Bank and in the other multilateral development banks (MDBs).[2] Its positive assessment recognized that the MDBs serve the national interest of a more stable and secure world, which can best be obtained in an open market-oriented international system. Insofar as MDBs encourage developing countries to participate on a permanent and self-sustaining basis, the report considers them a major vehicle for pursuing U.S. economic and strategic interests. The Baker initiative envisaged that the Bank take the lead in increased lending, supported by the regional development and private banks. The step-up in lending would be part of a broader program in which the borrowing countries would make specific growth-oriented policy changes.

In arriving at a positive judgment, the 1982 U.S. report explored the large extent to which the MDBs serve particular

U.S. objectives. The impact of the United States in the MDBs was greatest when objectives were well defined and also supported by other participants in the process (e.g., other governments, or World Bank management), whereas U.S. influence in the MDBs was much reduced when its objectives were poorly defined, inconsistent with other objectives, or opposed by other members. The report recommended that, in the future, the United States commit itself to well-defined objectives, seek support from one or more other parties, and back its position with substantial finance. U.S. budget considerations would give top priority to an increase in the callable capital of the IBRD but would also permit some nominal increase in U.S. contributions to IDA.

The 1982 U.S. report also recommended that support for the MDBs be designed to encourage adherence to free and open markets, emphasis on the private sector as a vehicle for growth, minimal government influence in development management, and assistance to the needy who are willing to help themselves. Realization of these objectives would have to come about gradually. The report also recognized that Bank operations are highly cost-effective. The lending policy recommendations of both the 1982 report and the October 1985 statement of Secretary Baker are consistent with the thrust of this book—in particular, the importance of linking World Bank operations with development policies, the greater stress on policy performance as against the realization of lending targets, and the importance of recovery in the private sector.

Marketing the Bank

Some conservative critics have argued that IBRD capital should not be increased at all. They hold instead that the Bank should become more exposed to market forces and less dependent on government support. Interested in giving the Bank a stronger private-sector orientation and opposed to increasing official support, these critics have proposed that IBRD capital be frozen or even rolled back. Along these lines, in a recent study undertaken for the Heritage Foundation, Dwight Phaup makes two proposals.

One is that the Bank's capital be rolled back to what is now paid in, while the statutory limitation—that loans outstanding and disbursed not exceed capital and reserves—be lifted altogether.[3] Further, callable capital would be rolled back in pace with maturation of the outstanding Bank bonds. Thus, the total authorized capital would be reduced from $81 billion to the paid-in level of $5.1 billion (as of June 1985) or $93 billion and $6.7 billion as of June 1986. The Bank's capital and reserves would be cut to about $8.8 billion, or 17 percent of its 1985 level. This cutback, according to Phaup, would remove the government subsidy granted to the Bank in the form of callable capital. However, in claiming that the high rating of Bank bonds is based on the callable capital, Phaup makes no allowance for the quality of the Bank's loan portfolio and its cautious management. Further, in his discussion he ignores the fact that the Bank has never suffered a default, has never had to make a call on its capital, and is managed in such a way that such calls are not likely in the future.

An alternative proposal, somewhat less restrictive, would freeze the Bank's capital. New lending would be restricted to repayments of outstanding loans plus new additions to reserves. Based on 1984 data, this proposal would require lending to be reduced to around $3.8 billion, or roughly one-third of total lending ($11.9 billion). Additional lending would be possible by selling new bonds without the backing of the Bank's callable capital or by selling Bank loans to the market or to governments interested in them for The aim of this proposal is an increase both in the role of private capital in financing developing countries and in the Bank's responsiveness to the foreign policy objectives of national governments (who would "buy" loans compatible with their objectives). Further, the Bank's lending program would become subject to a direct market test, while its policy stance in developing countries would also have to be more strongly in favor of private-sector interests.

These proposals seem inappropriate under prevailing conditions, given the possibilities in international credit markets. First, the restructuring of major debtor nations, the present low level of new private bank lending, and the cautious and innovative steps needed to bring back voluntary private lending call for a flexible and forthright posture by the World Bank, not a cutback of more than half its present level of lending. Second, cutbacks of this proportion—indeed, any cutback in official lending—would drive developing countries into isolation, and thus work against the interest of integrating world markets for capital, products, and services. Reducing the Bank's presence in developing countries would curtail its present and potential influence in favor of more rational economic policies and private-sector development. Third, making the Bank dependent on the sale of individual loans to governments would politicize it and damage its international stature so highly regarded by all its members, including the United States (as judged by the reports of the U.S. administration).[4] Finally, the claim that the proposal not to expand the Bank would economize on budget expenditures is plainly false. Apart from budget contributions for the capital increases agreed to in the past, no new budget resources are needed for further increases in capital (see chap. 8).

The foregoing does not deny the importance of continued rejuvenation of the Bank's market orientation. But a stronger market and private-sector orientation can best be served by building the Bank and encouraging the integration of LDCs into the global economy. On the other hand, some of the objectives of Phaup's proposals can be achieved over time by judicious adaptations in the Bank's financial and lending operations, changes that are already underway in many respects. In the years immediately ahead, the Bank can both expand its lending and become a more effective institution through a combination of measures:

First, maintaining and increasing the callable capital is essential and, given the Bank's record of management, would not result in any budget cost to governments. The callable capital is needed because buyers of IBRD bonds correctly perceive that lending for development is inherently risky. To remove the IBRD's capital backing could easily damage the Bank's ability to perform its basic functions: innovation, search for solutions to help resume or maintain a new growth momentum, and encouragement of private banks and investors to increase their capital flows to developing countries.

Second, it is important that the Bank stress new ways of raising resources that will economize on its own capital and stimulate private capital flows.

Third, the Bank's lending program should be based on consideration and execution of individual country programs that take account of alternative sources of finance, both private and official. Bilateral finance, even where politically motivated, would, of course, contribute to this process.

Fourth, the size and timing of a general increase in capital should be linked to the execution of programs for the major countries and to the use of alternative sources of finance.

Critics who favor a stronger market orientation also want the World Bank, and particularly IDA, to be more responsive to the political objectives of member governments. With this in mind, Phaup proposes that IDA replenishment and operations be replaced by a different procedure.[5] Instead of receiving advance allocations of government funds, IDA would, for a fee, prepare projects and then "sell" them to interested donors. To some extent this procedure is already being followed in the operation of the sub-Saharan Africa Facility. But making such a project-by-project procedure general would encumber the administration of IDA. After many years of IDA replenishment discussions, donor governments have reached a fairly firm understanding on the way IDA can best administer its resources. Moreover, while no new drastic changes are needed, IDA management can adapt its operations to different country conditions, with the assistance of the executive directors who are present full time to oversee the lending process.

In conclusion, the ways in which the Bank can become more responsive to market forces and and should continue to be tested and pursued. Present conditions in credit and capital markets call for a strong World Bank able to adapt its lending to circumstances in the borrowing countries. But the size and timing of the increase in capital can be made dependent on progress in the sale of loans, cofinancing, and effective operation of comprehensive and realistic country programs.

Public Opinion

Governments need widespread public support if they are to help carry out an expanding and constructive World Bank program. Such support is of special importance in the United States, which has long provided leadership in the Bank. And from the United States have come some of the most challenging ideas about reshaping the Bank and official assistance generally.

Surveys of public attitudes in the United States show that the public ranks foreign policy lowest in importance among official policies; U.S. foreign assistance receives a particularly dismal ranking. The public has much greater interest in domestic issues, such as the creation and protection of jobs, the plight of the farmer, and the maintenance of the value of the dollar. The East-West conflict is more important in the public mind than North-South collaboration. Foreign policy is a concern not of the common man but of the elite, the relatively rich, and the well educated.[6]

There is no overarching permanent coalition in the United States for public support for development, although many interested and influential parties participate in periodic meetings on the role of the World Bank. The International Development Conference, which meets every two years, brings together the various supporters of aid. Further, the recent formation of a Bretton Woods Committee of some 150 prominent leaders in business and other fields willing to speak out in favor of the Bank and the IMF is a welcome step forward. While this new group can be highly influential, one would hope that it will also attract younger leaders from *all* segments of the political spectrum. In June 1986, the Overseas Development Council organized a conference on the future of the Bank, with participation of bankers, academics, and foreign policy experts.[7]

In practice, however, as one congressional aide observed, the World Bank has neither outspoken enemies nor very good friends. It enjoys little grass-roots support. It is to most people a remote and unknown institution. What can it do to make itself better known and improve its image?

Dissemination of its experience, policies, and research findings can play an important role. But dissemination is extremely difficult, given the Bank's broad range of functions and the variety of regional and country problems it must address. The Bank's education programs are necessarily directed to a worldwide audience in both developed and developing countries. They seek to enhance the effectiveness and efficiency of development, promote global integration, train officials in LDCs, and influence the policies of industrial countries toward development. However, in the Bank's 1986 administrative budget, only about 5 percent of total is devoted to External Relations and the Economic Development Institute (EDI), the two Bank departments concerned with outside education; spending on public affairs and information is less than 2 percent of the total budget. A sharper focus of the Bank's dissemination and information and an increase in the resources devoted to them would be of interest to the international community.

The Bank's EDI has recently embarked on a new five-year program, which gives more attention to overall development policies. EDI has started to conduct seminars for senior government officials with a focus on structural adjustment in Africa. In 1986 it conducted or sponsored 105 courses (of which 85 percent were in cooperation with other training institutes). These courses had some 3,300 participants, 1,600 from the poorest countries. In the future, it could usefully give more attention to policy issues in major debtor and middle income countries and in China and India. For officials in these countries, the EDI could become an important and badly needed instrument for interchange of ideas on the nature of long-term structural adjustment, the conditions of success and failure of specific measures, and the prospects of trade and growth. For example, Latin American officials are interested in learning more about East Asian experiences, and African officials do not like to be treated in isolation from their counterparts in other LDCs.

Much of the Bank's very diverse publication program is addressed to the academic community and makes available unique source material to teachers and researchers. Its research has stimulated academic work on development and attracted economists to its staff. However, a greater part of the Bank's education efforts could be directed toward groups in the United States and elsewhere that have a common interest with the Bank: businesses and banks that share its international economic interests; humanitarian, church, and labor groups concerned with programs for food production and the improved productivity of broad layers of the population; and groups interested in the development of particular regions. In this effort the Bank can point to its work on health and education projects, and on small industry, agriculture, and industrial productivity.

The Bank has already begun to pay more attention to private voluntary agencies (PVOs), many of which perform highly cost-effective services and receive broad, popular support. World Bank and PVO operations can reinforce each other in many ways. The Bank can benefit from and supplement the education programs of PVOs aimed at broadening support for specific aspects of development. Collaboration with PVOs is no simple task, however, given their large numbers and diversity. One hopes that dialogue, now conducted regularly, will result in greater PVO participation in the Bank's projects.[8]

Finally, the Bank's public information has done little to reach out to groups that believe government and welfare programs have become increasingly unproductive in creating new wealth and higher incomes. In this context, several aspects of the Bank's operations deserve better explanation and dissemination. The Bank has not yet published a clear and comprehensive statement on the evolution and present thrust of its policies—for example, how it assesses the policy performance of developing countries and how it operates in different country situations; what conditions are attached to its different lending instruments and how it implements them; and how it supports and enhances private capital flows and private-sector development. It has also not yet published its views on the nature and application of its own country programs and the specific links between major lending operations, the policies of recipient countries, and the simultaneous actions of other lenders.

In short, to muster support from the official puarters and public opinion, the Bank can do much to improve understanding of its policies and procedures. This challenging task deserves more resources than it has received so far.

10

Facing the Future

WHEN BARBER B. CONABLE became president of the World Bank in July 1986, the Bank faced the need for expanded action in three areas:

• It was generally recognized that to overcome or at least reduce the lingering adverse impact of the 1982 debt crisis, a growth-oriented strategy had to be adopted, supported by significant policy initiatives in both industrial and developing debtor countries and by the provision of new long-term finance. In the view of several observers, the situation called for a combination of patience, persistence, and innovative action.[1]

• Many of the poorest countries, especially in sub-Saharan Africa, had started to adopt more market-oriented policies. In addition, IDA and bilateral aid agencies were taking steps to make their assistance more effective. But the problems they faced were deep-seated, and continued concessionary aid was expected to be necessary for many years.

• In both the middle-income and the poorest countries, the private sector, which accounted for at least three-quarters of total output, was deeply depressed. But no growth strategy could succeed without the encouragement and support of the thousands of independent farmers and businessmen in the private sector.

The Bank's external environment is now drastically different from what it was in the fifties and sixties, when it first developed its lending standards. The often sharper differentiation among the developing countries calls for special attention to the different categories of countries. In addition, LDCs have become more integrated in the global economy and are more vulnerable to external fluctuations in interest rates and export prices. There is also a much wider awareness of the importance of market forces and of the limitations of direct government intervention.

The Bank is well equipped to make vital contributions in all three of the areas specified above, although, to do so, it must adapt its policies and organization to the new circumstances and significantly upgrade the effectiveness and quality of its economic work. But, even if it does so, the Bank—as part of a complex and closely knit international financial system—has only limited freedom of action. It is the private banks who are now the principal creditors in most middle-income countries.

The World Bank has built a strong record of adaptation to changing circumstances. It first established its credit standing and credibility by evolving the project concept in its lending for development. It helped many countries in preparing projects in both infrastructure and directly productive sectors. It broke new ground by helping set up local development banks that were able to attract domestic and external funds and channel them into numerous small businesses in industry and agriculture. It undertook major international projects such as the development of the Indus River Basin. Over the years it significantly changed the approach and policy of its principal lending activities in infrastructure, agriculture, and industry. It has steadily given top priority to various aspects of agricultural development. In the seventies it made special efforts to support agricultural research, rural development, and small industries. It helped develop an analytical framework for assessing the compatibility of equity and growth. And when the price of energy rose sharply in the seventies, the Bank greatly expanded its support for production and conservation of energy.

In all these activities the Bank had to innovate and develop new tools and approaches, building on available knowledge in both developing and industrial countries. It is true, however, that in the process of change the Bank itself has become more a follower than a leader. And as its operations have grown in size and complexity, it has also become slower and more cumbersome. This is borne out by the Bank's record during the debt crisis and by its reluctant attention to the growing concern with environmental issues. The Bank's sometimes lethargic behavior in recent years poses a special challenge to Conable.

As president (1981–86), Tom Clausen recognized the wide diversity of problems the Bank faces and the nature of the contributions it can make toward longer-run solutions. In 1981 the Bank proposed a strategy for dealing with the crisis of hunger, instability, and decline in sub-Saharan Africa. But the Bank's response to the urgent needs of Africa appears to have come at the expense of action elsewhere.

While pursuing its African strategy, the Bank tended to downplay the ramifications of the external debt crisis, which primarily affected the middle-income countries. Until Conable took over as president in mid-1986, the Bank had kept an unduly low profile on international debt issues. It had adopted a special program for accelerating loan disbursements in 1983, but by mid-1987 it had not yet come up with a comprehensive strategy for overcoming the burdens of excessive debt, a strategy that is badly needed by all parties concerned. The Bank's general analysis, as reflected in the *World Development Report 1985*, was essentially confined to a description of the workings of the marketplace. However, reliance on market forces had brought on the debt crisis in the first place and has not yet resolved it satisfactorily. The report did not try to develop new analytical approaches or suggest a new strategy for dealing with debt.

The Bank's timid posture on international debt issues stood in sharp contrast to its own activities and analyses in earlier years. As early as the fifties, the Bank had provided advice to countries (including Mexico) on their management of external borrowing and made cautious borrowing policies a condition for additional Bank lending. In the early sixties it pioneered an in-depth analysis of the inter-relations between debt and growth.[2] It drew attention to the "critical interest rate," concluding that countries would soon encounter severe debt servicing difficulties if they borrowed at interest rates far above their export growth rate or the return on investments—a warning that sadly proved true in 1982.

The widespread and severe malaise in the private sector calls for a well-directed and comprehensive strategy designed to remove present obstacles to vigorous growth. Under Clausen, the Bank dealt with many elements in such a program, including policy changes designed to make enterprises more efficient, a better balance between the public and private sectors, a restructuring of state enterprises, rationalization of domestic credit policies, and suitable infrastructure investments. But until 1987 the Bank had not combined these various elements into a unified, overall strategy for private-sector development.

At the same time, the Bank's affiliate, the IFC, is in the midst of a five-year expansion program (1985–90) with operations projected to grow by 7 percent per annum. IFC focuses both on mobilizing external finance for individual private enterprises and on restructuring enterprises to which it has lent in the past. In addition, it assists in developing indigenous capital markets. It also has undertaken studies of industrial investment incentives although it has not yet had much influence on country policies. But the IFC is run quite separately from the World Bank. Urgently needed comprehensive action on private-sector development would require much more intensive collaboration, if not full integration of the work of the two institutions.

Agenda for Action

The severity and long-term nature of the problems faced by both the poorest countries and the major debtor economies make the Bank the logical institution to provide essential leadership. Indeed, the direction now needed most might best come from a multilateral development institution, with help from others that thus far have also been active in working out financing arrangements for the major debtors. As is evident from articles and staff reports, the Bank has the ingredients of a comprehensive debt strategy.[3] As of mid-1986, with the assistance of the IMF, the regional development banks, and others, it faced the task of orchestrating and enacting an international program designed to resolve the debt crisis.

As an experienced long-term investment bank, the World Bank has the technical capacity to mobilize an increasing flow of capital, both private and public, and put it to good use. It can play a central role in restructuring the economies of developing countries through support of major investments, modernization, rehabilitation, and expansion of manufacturing industry, and through rationalization of public-sector management and policies. The Bank can be most effective if it can adapt its own lending to the longer-term requirements of borrowing countries and to their willingness to pursue open, growth-oriented policies.

To have a lasting impact, policy reform must be genuinely indigenous and based on broad domestic political commitment. It cannot be governed by rigid formulas imposed by outsiders. Fortunately, the Bank's policy assistance has usually recognized domestic diversity and has been carried out in a nonconfrontational and cooperative spirit. Even so, the

Bank has been tough in insisting on conditions that are essential to the success of its loan projects and programs. In widening its role, it could publish guidelines that govern its operations, for use by its officers as well as by borrowers and other lending agencies. It issued such guidelines in the sixties, but they have not since been fully updated.

The Bank makes many different kinds of loans. Some are for narrowly defined projects, mostly specific investments; these are of special interest to the least-developed countries, which often lack well-functioning institutions so important to better performance. Others are broader sector loans, which address issues of strategy, policy, and investment priorities in particular sectors (e.g., education, infrastructure, or agriculture) and help finance projects in those sectors. Program loans (or structural adjustment loans) cut across sectors and are linked to particular policies designed to improve efficiency, project preparation, and execution of long-term investments.

The distinction between project and program loans, which so often comes up in discussions of World Bank lending policy, is rather unimportant in both practice and substance. Instead, the critical issue is how the Bank can best deliver its technical and policy assistance and make sure its loan funds are well spent. Despite many changes in the Bank's loan mix over the years, there is an essential continuity in the Bank's fundamental objective of increasing both domestic and external resources devoted to efficient development. But the Bank need not go overboard in making balance-of-payments loans, which are in the area of IMF expertise.

Given the wide variety of its lending instruments, since the late sixties the Bank has regularly prepared programs for external lending to individual countries. These country programs provide a comprehensive strategy for the design and sequencing of lending and other operations. They also specify the extent and terms of external finance suitable for dealing with the country's problems and prospects, as well as basic issues of creditworthiness and development policy. These issues are addressed in discussions with the recipient country and in the implementation of the loan program. Unfortunately, the Bank has not placed these country programs in the center of action and negotiation between the debtor countries and the various sources of external finance, including the IMF, the commerical banks, and the regional development banks. It would do well to make more systematic and operational use of its country programs in discussions with other providers of finance about long-term financing needs and development policies of individual countries.

Formulation and execution of country programs require close cooperation between the Bank's loan officers and its economic officers, with the latter assuming full operational responsibility for the Bank's policy assistance. At the end of Clausen's presidency in mid-1986, internal organization still had to be streamlined to enable the Bank to act expeditiously yet competently in difficult situations. Conable has now undertaken the most thorough staff reorganization in the Bank's forty-year history. One hopes that the new organization will sharpen the Bank's focus on development issues and enable senior Bank management to give strong direction to preparing country programs and to discussions with members countries and other lenders. One would also expect that, as the Bank strengthens its operational attention to development policies, its Board of Directors will start reviewing the Bank's country programs so as to be able to consider individual loans in the context of a broader strategy. Finally, the Bank can help build a more adequate analytical approach to adjustment in a framework of growth as well as to reduction of debt burdens in a way both realistic and compatible with development needs. It can do so best by drawing on its own expertise and experience and by more closely integrating its economic research and operational work.

Working with Other Sources of Finance

In executing an expanding lending program, the Bank will need to maintain close and effective working relations with other sources of finance. In present circumstances, the Bank's working relations with the IMF and the commercial banks are of special importance.

The debt crisis and the ensuing scarcity of capital have given new urgency to the Bank's catalytic functions, through which it encourages and facilitates finance from other providers of long-term loans and investments. The Bank can act as a catalyst in the full range of its own operations, including lending as well as technical and policy assistance. Besides its own operations strategy, instruments that are particularly useful are coordinating external assistance and cofinancing with other lenders.

The World Bank has long provided coordination of external capital flows to LDCs, including organizing and chairing aid consortia (e.g., for Bangladesh, India, and Pakistan) and consultative groups. Compared with the sixties and seventies, coordination is now even more important because of the much greater scarcity of long-term finance and the larger number of banks and official agencies involved.

As is evident from the experience with the Bank's oldest consultative group, that for Colombia, coordination arrangements have to be adapted periodically to the changing requirements of the participants. In 1982, the Colombian government chaired its own group for the first time, and a large number of commercial banks from sixteen countries participated in the meeting.

In recent years, the Bank has conducted coordinating meetings for India and the other countries of South Asia, for the smaller recipients of IDA credits, and for Ghana, the Philippines, and Zaire. It has not held meetings on the provision of long-term finance for the major debtor nations, and it could take a more active role in mobilizing and coordinating long-term finance to benefit a new growth strategy to resolve the debt crisis. But to make this happen, the Bank's coordination policies must be adapted to new conditions, including making the meetings of greater interest to commercial banks. The Bank will need to assess continuously the effectiveness of its arrangements in mobilizing finance, broadening support for policy reform, and improving the use of aid.

In making its own operations more effective, the Bank will need to deepen and broaden its working relations with the IMF. The Fund and the Bank each have a distinct role in resolving the debt crisis and improving the performance of the developing countries. At the same time, their operations complement each other, with the Fund concentrating on monetary and exchange rate policies and supporting balance-of-payments finance, and the Bank concentrating on structural policies and long-term investment finance. In 1982–85, the Fund swiftly took the lead in counteracting the initial effects of the debt crisis. Its understandings with member countries have important implications for longer-term structural policies and hence also complement the Bank's country programs.

The management and staff of the two institutions have now started to work together more closely. But much of their collaboration has been aimed at avoiding conflict rather than working out new approaches. A global strategy would be enhanced if the Fund and the Bank were to operate in a more unified fashion, both in their country programs and in their more general analysis, such as in the use of macroeconomic and sector policies in promoting long-term growth.

The World Bank can still go some way to induce the commercial banks to make a more positive contribution to the LDCs. As the most important creditors of the major debtor countries, the commercial banks' attitude toward restructuring existing debt and providing new finance is critical to the viability of new initiatives. But in recent years these banks have not provided new finance for the major debtor countries; yet they have received interest payments from them exceeding $40 billion annually. Any growth strategy will be handicapped by continuation of outward transfers of such magnitude.

In the past, the commercial banks often lent without taking into account the need for essential adjustment measures in the borrowing countries. Neither was much of their lending linked to high-priority investments. In the future, the impact of private lenders will be more favorable if they pay more attention to the signals given by the Fund and the Bank. In lending for development projects, the commercial banks can benefit by operating in the framework of the country programs of the World Bank and by increasing their participation in lending for the execution of these programs. Coordination and information provided by the Bank can help both private banks and private investors gear their operations more closely to the requirements of the developing countries and help the banks adopt a more normal lending posture.

Financing the Bank

The World Bank should increase its lending at a brisk pace if it is to help start and sustain a process of new growth in the global economy. It will have to meet the demand for financing of new investment and modernization, encourage countries to open up their economies and be come more efficient, exercise its catalytic functions, and make up for the slack in private lending. The pace of its lending, of course, will have to depend intimately on the adoption of growth-oriented policies in both the industrial and developing countries.

The main thrust of World Bank expansion in the years ahead will be in the IBRD, which lends on market-related terms, rather than in IDA, the Bank's arm for concessionary finance fed almost exclusively by cash contributions of the industrial countries. An increase in IBRD lending of about 10 percent per year to $20–$25 billion annually in the early nineties will require a substantial increase in capital. Most new finance for the IBRD is obtained through the sale of bonds to private investors and others. The IBRD has an outstanding record of managing the sale of its bonds—some $10 billion annually in recent years—through diversification over many markets and currencies. But the quality of its bonds is crucially dependent on the backing of the Bank's guarantee capital. Besides the IBRD paid-in capital and reserves, the share of the callable capital subscribed (but not paid in) by the industrial countries is of particular interest to the bond markets. This market judgment prevails despite the facts that the Bank has never suffered a default on its loans and that the likelihood is remote that the IBRD would have to call on its capital because of widespread defaults. The IBRD itself has grown into a strong financial institution, with liquid resources over $20 billion, profits exceeding $1.2 billion, and earnings on average equity over 13 percent in 1986.

The Bank has to take various steps to make the most of its existing capital (SDR 78.6 billion in June 1986; or $92.6 billion, of which $77.5 billion was subscribed and $6.7 billion was paid in). It can do so by selling part of its loan portfolio, seeking greater participation by others in financing its loan projects and programs, and promoting innovations in its lending techniques and in the use of its guarantee of loans made by others. But these steps, some advocated by conservative critics, do not lessen the need for a general capital increase in the next few years of at least $40–$50 billion, and even more were the IBRD to help reduce the burden of interest payments on existing or new external debt. The case for increasing the IBRD capital is strengthened by the fact that the Bank needs no new cash from governments. Thus, the cost of a capital increase to their budgets is minimal. Even so, in permitting the Bank's capital to increase, governments will have to make a political decision to underwrite an expanding level of IBRD operations.

IDA is the single most important source of loans on concessionary terms—that is, terms softer than those available on the market. The poorest countries, especially Bangladesh and those in sub-Saharan Africa, depend on IDA assistance for making their development efforts more effective and efficient. Throughout 1981–87, IDA has been committing new credits at a rather stable level of slightly more than $3 billion per year. In 1986 IDA operations were supplemented by those of the Special Facility for Sub-Saharan Africa, administered by the World Bank. (The facility has $1.6 billion in total resources, of which $782 million were committed in 1986.)

During Clausen's tenure as president, Bank management tried hard—some think too hard—to increase IDA resources. In fall 1986, tentative agreement was reached to enable IDA to operate at a commitment level of $4 billion per year for the three years starting July 1987. In real terms, this would about equal what IDA and the Sub-Saharan Africa Facility have been able to commit in the previous three years. IDA will have to devote an increasing share to the poorest African countries and Bangladesh and relatively less to China and India (which together received 34 percent of total IDA credits in 1986). Shifting World Bank operations in China and India from IDA to the IBRD further underlines the importance of increasing IBRD capital.

Conditions in many of the poorest countries may make concessionary assistance to them necessary for many years. Indeed, in some of these countries present conditions are significantly more difficult than those encountered when IDA first began operations—for example, in Colombia and Korea during the sixties. World Bank efforts to make assistance to Africa more effective would be greatly enhanced by its continuing ability to commit new IDA credits.

The processes of keeping IBRD capital at an adequate level

and of periodically replenishing IDA resources have become difficult and often controversial. Perhaps this cannot be avoided. But the Bank's cause would be strengthened by more open and systematic consideration of its country programs and by close monitoring of their results. The possibility of convincing skeptics is stronger when one can point to the evidence of concrete country cases rather than to general reasoning and hypothetical projections.

Support for the Bank

As the World Bank gears up for a larger and more effective role, its management will need to be responsive to the views of both developing and industrial countries. Conversely, the Bank will be hard put to do a better job unless member governments give it their full support.

It would be hard to deny that the Bank's operations in many ways reinforce the policies of the industrial countries and the interests of the developing countries. The Bank is instrumental in promoting growth in the LDCs and their integration into the global economy. The developing countries themselves are a major market for industrial country exports.

In its operations over the years, the Bank has followed the policy orientation of donor countries as well as of developing countries such as India and Brazil, in that it has favored the mobilization and efficient use of resources. Rather than supporting government intervention, as some critics have argued, it has encouraged rational price incentives for agriculture and industry, and autonomy of both private and public enterprises; and it has discouraged excessive protection and uneconomic investments. It has conducted its operations in a businesslike manner, and it can expand them substantially without increasing personnel or imposing new burdens on government budgets. All these are strong points in its favor when governments of industrial countries come to consider expansion of the World Bank.

A more positive attitude of the developing countries is especially important to the reorientation of the World Bank. The Bank's policy assistance and coordination activities must be seen as a cooperative venture, with the LDCs taking the lead. But despite World Bank efforts to increase its lending commitments and disbursements, some LDC spokesmen, in United Nations forums and public discourse, have often been critical of the Bank and given it only lukewarm support. In meetings of the Bank's Executive Board, some representatives of the LDCs have objected to discussion of country programs and lending strategy. They have, in effect, isolated the board from management and staff consideration of Bank lending in the context of a broader country policies and priorities. One would hope that, in the future, LDC directors would cooperate more fully in the reorientation of Bank activities so essential to its role in promoting a stronger strategy for growth, and that discussion in the Bank's board can continue to be free of rhetoric and focus on action and financial support for development. It is true that representation on the board is weighted by countries' shares in the Bank's capital, giving the LDCs a minority position. But in practice, decisions are made not through voting or political confrontation, but through informal discussion and consent arrived at in a cooperative spirit.

Governments will need widespread public support if they are to make a political commitment to an expanding Bank program. But the Bank is a rather unknown and remote institution to most people, and it has very few friends. To muster support, it will have to address its critics on both the right and the left itself. It must pay more attention to the views of the many groups and private voluntary organizations interested in development or concerned with eradicating hunger, poverty, and social injustice. One would hope that volunteers will be given an opportunity to have increasing participation in the Bank's operations.

The Bank can do more to explain the nature and objectives of its operations to various audiences around the world. Admittedly, this is an extremely complex task, requiring a highly competent staff and an increased budget. In this effort, the Bank's public affairs department and its Economic Development Institute, as well as dissemination of its research results, will be critical. It may also be possible to induce private research institutes to devote more resources to understanding the Bank's work and to helping its policies evolve.

The Bank's educational and research activities can be highly cost-effective in improving global understanding of development issues and helping achieve some of the Bank's main objectives: the increase of financial and technical resources for development and their effective application in many different circumstances, the widening of the Bank's role as an intermediary between capital markets and developing countries, and the strengthening of collaboration between domestic and foreign investors.

With wider public understanding and support, the Bank can go steadily ahead in the role for which its purposes and experience uniquely fit it. The challenge before the World Bank today is to live up to its potential as the best qualified of all international institutions to mobilize the resources, public and private, domestic and foreign, which are needed for a growing world economy whose benefits are shared by people everywhere.

Epilogue

Since this book was written, president Barber Conable has undertaken a major reorganization of the World Bank. The Bank's activities are now grouped under four senior vice-presidents, one each for operations; finance; policy, planning, and research; and administration. The new structure's purpose is to streamline working procedures, simplify supervision, and, generally, increase efficiency. It is expected that 10 to 20 percent of the Bank's professional staff will retire or resign as a result.

Yet, even in its new shape, responsibility within the Bank remains divided in some key areas. For example, research on the international debt problem and action on the debts of individual countries continue to fall under different vice-presidents. And two units crucial to the Bank's ability to explain itself to the outside world, the Economic Development Institute and the public affairs department, are no longer linked, as they were before, under one senior officer. Thus strong presidential leadership will be required to assure that the Bank functions at full effectiveness.

The tasks and issues before the Bank, described in this book, have not been affected by the reorganization. They remain urgent and demanding.

July 1987

Notes

Chapter 1.
The Critics of the World Bank

1. An early critic in this school is Teresa Hayter, *Aid as Imperialism* (Harmondsworth, Middlesex, England: Penguin Books, 1971). For a recent collection of criticism of this sort, see Jill Torrie, ed., *Banking on Poverty: The Global Impact of the IMF and the World Bank* (Toronto: "Between the Lines," 1984); see also Cheryl Payer, *The World Bank: A Critical Analysis* (New York: Monthly Review Press, 1983).

2. Greater LDC representation on the staff was one recommendation in Escott Reid, *Strengthening the World Bank* (Chicago: Adlai Stevenson Institute, 1973). Much progress has been made since this book was written.

3. See *North-South: A Program for Survival*, Report of the Independent Commission on International Development Issues under the Chairmanship of Willy Brandt (Cambridge, Mass.: MIT Press, 1980).

4. The discussion draws on P.T. Bauer, *Equality, the Third World and Economic Delusion* (Cambridge, Mass.: Harvard University Press, 1981), especially chap. 5, "Foreign Aid and Its Hydra-Headed Rationalization." Bauer's "Remembrance of Studies Past: Retracing First Steps," in *Pioneers in Development*, ed. Gerald M. Meier and Dudley Seers (New York: Oxford University Press, 1984), deals primarily with his early studies on the development effects of commercial forces. The general discussion on aid effectiveness in E. Dwight Phaup, *The World Bank: How It Can Serve U.S. Interests* (Washington: Heritage Foundation, 1984), largely follows Bauer's arguments.

5. See "Does Aid Help Development?" in *World Development Report 1985* (New York: Oxford University Press, 1985), 101-105; Anne

O. Krueger and Vernon W. Ruttan, "The Development Impact of Economic Assistance to LDCs" (Washington: USAID, 1983); and the study on aid effectiveness for the Bank-Fund Development Committee, *Report of the Task Force on Concessional Flows* (Washington: World Bank, 1985).

6. See Keith Marsden and Alan Roe, "The Political Economy of Foreign Aid," *Labour and Society* 8, 1 (1983) (also in World Bank Reprint Series, no. 256).

7. For early examples of the Bank's support for decentralized planning, see Albert Waterston, *Development Planning: Lessons of Experience* (Baltimore, Md.: Johns Hopkins University Press, 1965).

8. See "Operations Evaluation" in chap. 6 of this volume, and *World Development Report 1985*, 103.

9. See, e.g., Phaup, *The World Bank*, 36.

10. See Melvyn B. Krauss, "The World Bank Off Course," in Allan H. Meltzer, ed., *International Lending and the IMF* (Washington: Heritage Foundation, 1983).

11. See Robert L. Ayres, *Banking on the Poor* (Cambridge, Mass.: MIT Press, 1983); and *Focus on Poverty* (Washington: World Bank, 1983).

Chapter 2.
The World Bank Family: A Retrospective Look

1. Given the criticism that the less developed countries were absent from the conference, it is worth noting that many LDCs, including China, India, and most Latin American countries, participated in the deliberations. Some of those present, indeed—such as India and the Philippines—were not yet independent.

2. Article I of Articles of Agreement of the International Bank for Reconstruction and Development (IBRD). The articles are a model of clarity and general applicability. Over the years they have been changed only in minor ways. They have been supplemented by Articles of Agreement for the IFC (1955) and for IDA (1960).

3. The Bank's first twenty-five years are described in Edward S. Mason and Robert E. Asher, *The World Bank Since Bretton Woods* (Washington: Brookings Institution, 1973). On the early years, see Davidson Sommers, "An Institution Emerges," *Finance and Development* 21, 2 (1984): 30.

4. The author benefited from a discussion with Harold N. Graves on George Woods' contributions. See also *Partners in Development*,

Report of the Commission on International Development, Lester B. Pearson, Chairman (New York and London: Praeger, 1969).

5. D. Avramovic and Assoc., *Economic Growth and External Debt* (Baltimore, Md.: Johns Hopkins University Press, 1965), and John de Wilde et al., *Experiences with Agricultural Development in Tropical Africa* (Baltimore, Md.: Johns Hopkins University Press, 1967).

6. William Clark, "McNamara at the World Bank," *Foreign Affairs* 60, 1 (1981): 167-184; and A.M. Kamarck, "Letter to the Editor: McNamara's Bank," *Foreign Affairs* 60, 4 (1982): 951.

7. Included in poverty-oriented lending are rural development (15 percent of total IBRD/IDA lending in 1979-81); water supply and sewage (6.7 percent); urban development and small-scale industry (5.1 percent); and education, health, and nutrition (2.9 percent). From World Bank, *Focus on Poverty*, 1983 edition.

Chapter 3.
The Bank's Record

1. See Montague Yudelman, "Agricultural Lending by the Bank 1974-84," *Finance and Development* 21, 4 (1984). The project cycle and the Bank's work in agriculture and other sectors are described in Warren C. Baum and Stokes M. Tolbert, *Investing in Development: Lessons of World Bank Experience* (Washington: World Bank; New York: Oxford University Press, 1985).

2. See "Agricultural Research," a Sector Policy Paper (Washington: World Bank, 1981). The history of the CGIAR can be found in Warren C. Baum, *Partners Against Hunger* (Washington: World Bank, 1986).

3. See *Financing Adjustment with Growth in Sub-Saharan Africa, 1986#90* (Washington: World Bank, 1986), 28.

4. See Mason and Asher, *The World Bank Since Bretton Woods*, 610-627, and Pieter Lieftinck, A. Robert Sadove, and Thomas C. Creyke, *Water and Power Resources of West Pakistan: A Study in Sector Planning*, 3 vols. (Baltimore, Md.: Johns Hopkins University Press, 1969).

5. "Tropical Forests: A Call for Action," report by an international task force convened by the World Bank, the World Resources Institute, and the UNDP (Washington: World Bank, 1985).

6. James A. Lee, *The Environment, Public Health and Human Ecology: Considerations of Economic Development* (Baltimore, Md.: Johns Hopkins University Press, 1986).

7. Energy lending includes oil, gas, coal, electric power, and other

subsectors (fuel wood, alcohol, refinery conversion, and energy conservation).

8. See *The Energy Transition in Developing Countries* (Washington: World Bank, 1983). This study reflects the Bank's experience in energy lending and analysis over the previous ten years.

9. Edward R. Fried and Henry D. Owen, eds., *The Future Role of the World Bank* (Washington: Brookings Institution, 1982), 31.

10. For example, in Egypt, India, Jamaica, Morocco, Portugal, and Turkey. See *The Energy Transition in Developing Countries.*

11. For example, in Bangladesh, Egypt, Morocco, and Tanzania.

12. Exploration and production agreements have been signed with Madagascar, Mali, and Mauritania.

13. See, in particular, Bela Balassa and Assoc., *The Structure of Protection in Developing Countries* (Baltimore, Md.: Johns Hopkins University Press, 1971) and *Development Strategies in Semi-Industrial Economies* (Baltimore, Md.: Johns Hopkins University Press, 1982).

14. Lending for education averaged $589 million in 1982–84, or 4.1 percent of total. Most Bank loans now include training and education components as part of the project; these components, together with education loans, added up to $790 million in 1983, or 5.5 percent of total Bank lending (and $902 million, or 6.9 percent of the total, in 1982).

15. World Bank, *World Development Report 1984* (New York: Oxford University Press, 1984) and "Population Growth and Economic and Social Development," addresses by A.W. Clausen (Washington: World Bank, 1984).

16. The urgency of population policies is emphasized in Robert S. McNamara, "Time Bomb or Myth: The Population Problem," *Foreign Affairs* 62, 5 (1984): 1107-1131.

Chapter 4.
The Changing International Environment

1. In this study, the poorest countries have per capita GNP (1983) below $400, the lower-middle-income countries are in the $400–$1600 range, and the upper-middle-income countries have per capita GNP above $1600. Cf. *World Development Report 1985*, 174.

2. These data are from the 1984 Report of the Chairman of the DAC (Development Assistance Committee) (Paris: Organization for

Economic Cooperation and Development [OECD], 1985), tables II.A.1 and II.C.1.

3. See *Development and Debt Service: Dilemma of the 1980s* (Washington: World Bank, 1986).

Chapter 5.
Critical Issues Facing the Bank

1. For full discussion of Africa's plight, see *Accelerated Development in Sub-Saharan Africa (Washington: World Bank, 1981), Toward Sustained Development in Sub-Saharan Africa* (Washington: World Bank, 1984), and *Financing Adjustment with Growth in Sub-Saharan Africa (1986–90)* (Washington: World Bank, 1986).

2. See *Toward Sustained Development in Sub-Saharan Africa*, 13.

3. See *Accelerated Development in Sub-Saharan Africa*, 19.

4. See table 1. Private voluntary organizations registered with USAID had programs exceeding $1 billion in 1982.

5. See Vittorio Masoni, "Non-Governmental Organizations and Development," *Finance and Development* 22, 3 (1985).

6. See, e.g., the review of projections in William R. Cline, *International Debt: Systemic Risk and Policy Response* (Washington: Institute for International Economics; Cambridge, Mass.: MIT Press, 1984), chap. 8.

7. See International Monetary Fund (IMF), *World Economic Outlook, 1984* (Occasional Paper 27). The Fund's projection of imports by developing countries suggests that they may have to fall below the level indicated by the relation between imports and output in the past. Private credit is projected to increase by 3 percent per annum in real terms as against domestic growth of about 4 percent (which may be 5 to 6 percent in some countries, such as Brazil). Official development assistance (concessionary credit) is expected to remain constant in real terms, but private direct investment is projected to grow by more than 5 percent per year in real terms (starting from a low base). The IMF's projections do not consider the external finance requirements of developing countries and how they should be met. Projections of capital flows to debtor countries are summarized in Donald R. Lessard and John Williamson, *Financial Intermediation Beyond the Debt Crisis* (Washington: Institute for International Economics, 1985).

8. See Barend A. de Vries, "International Ramifications of the External Debt Situation," *The AMEX Bank Review* Special Papers no.

8, November 1983 (also in World Bank Reprint Series, no. 294).

9. See *World Development Report 1985*, 64 and 65. The increase in total external debt during 1973–82 may be compared with the cumulative current account deficits (net of changes in reserves and direct foreign investment) in 1974–82. The increase in debt accounts for only 18 percent of the deficit in Argentina, 58 percent in Chile, and 37 percent in Mexico, as against 96 percent in Brazil. In Mexico this percentage declined rapidly in 1978–82, suggesting increasing external financing of capital flight (cf. Leopoldo Solis and Ernesto Zedillo, "The Foreign Debt of Mexico," in *International Debt and the Developing Countries*, ed. Gordon W. Smith and John T. Cuddington (Washington: World Bank, 1985).

10. The Bank's role in restructuring was explained by Ernest Stern in a speech to the International Conference on LDC Financing sponsored by the Federal Reserve Bank of New York (May 1984). See also Barend A. de Vries, "Restructuring Debtor Economies," *Journal of International Affairs* 38, 1 (1984).

11. World Bank, a collection of articles prepared for publication in *Finance and Development* (1981).

12. See Jean-Loup Dherse, "Moving Toward Privatization in Developing Countries," *The Bank's World*, April 1986.

13. In the seventies the Bank lent to Brazil to develop several capital-intensive industries including steel, fertilizer, petrochemical, and metal processing.

14. Samuel Paul, "Privatization and the Public Sector," *Finance and Development* 21, 4 (1984).

15. See Stephen Guisinger, *Investment Incentives and Performance Requirements* (New York: Praeger, 1985).

16. See "The Bank Group and the Private Sector," in Mason and Asher, *The World Bank Since Bretton Woods*, 743-749.

Chapter 6.
Linking Bank Lending with Policy Reform

1. It is also possible that the government is the borrower and that the activities of the project entity are set forth in a separate project agreement.

2. In discussions leading to the U.S. Bretton Woods Act of 1946, the World Bank was conceived as a conservative, market-related institution, which could provide long-term stabilization loans. These were thought of as similar to prewar private bank loans made to

rebuild the reserves of war-torn countries, and thus as rather different from World Bank loans tied to reconstruction or development programs. See Joseph Gold, "The Relationship Between the IMF and the World Bank," *Creighton Law Review* 15, 2 (1981–82): 510-511; Sidney Dell, "A Note on Stabilization and the World Bank," *World Development* 12, 2 (1984): 163-167; and Mason and Asher, *The World Bank Since Bretton Woods*, 25 and chap. 9. The early discussions on the World Bank Charter are reviewed in Robert W. Oliver, "Early Plans for a World Bank," *Princeton Studies in International Finance*, no. 29 (Princeton, N.J.: Princeton University, 1971).

3. See Barend A. de Vries, *The Philippines: Industrial Development Strategy and Policies* (Washington: World Bank, 1980); the government's statement is on pp. vii-ix.

4. See Pierre M. Landell-Mills, "Structural Adjustment Lending: Early Experience," *Finance and Development* 18, 4 (1981); Stanley Please, *The Hobbled Giant: Essays on the World Bank* (Boulder, Colo.: Westview Press, 1984), chap. 3; and Ernest Stern, "World Bank Financing of Structural Adjustment," in *IMF Conditionality*, ed. John Williamson (Washington: Institute for International Economics, 1983). In 1980–85, the Bank made 32 SALs to 17 countries (totaling $4.5 billion) and 37 sector adjustment loans to 26 countries (totaling $3.8 billion); see Clausen's speech to the 1985 Annual Meeting of IBRD-IMF Governors. An overview of Bank lending instruments is given in the Bank's 1985 Annual Report, table 3-1 (p. 50).

5. Gerald M. Alter, "World Bank Goals in Project Lending," *Finance and Development* 15, 2 (1978), explains how project loans can be designed to serve broad objectives.

6. The Special Assistance Program (1983–85) had the following elements: (a) expanded structural adjustment lending; (b) sector adjustment support (e.g., for export development); and (c) increase in the share of project cost covered by certain loans.

7. See, e.g., the Sector Policy Papers, published by the World Bank, on Agricultural Research (1981), Development Finance Companies (1976), Education (1980), Employment and the Development of Small Enterprises (1978), and Health (1980). Sector Policy Papers are not available on all sectors.

8. See, e.g., Hugh Collier, *Developing Electric Power: Thirty Years of World Bank Experience* (Baltimore, Md.: Johns Hopkins University Press, 1984).

9. The work of Bank economists is described in George B. Baldwin, "Economics and Economists in the World Bank," in *Economists in International Agencies*, ed. A.W. Coats (New York: Praeger, 1986).

The Bank's approach to economic work and evaluation of country policies in the sixties is described by Irving S. Friedman and Andrew M. Kamarck, *Some Aspects of the Economic Philosophy of the World Bank* (Washington: World Bank, 1968); see also Andrew M. Kamarck, "The Appraisal of Country Economic Performance," in *Economic Development and Cultural Change* 18 (January 1970).

10. IBRD lending policies in the early sixties are described in *The World Bank: Policies and Operations*, chap. 5; "Major Operational Policies" (IBRD: April 1962, amended to 30 June 1963, and earlier issues).

11. See Mason and Asher, *The World Bank Since Bretton Woods*, chap. 13, "Leverage and Performance."

12. Krueger pointed to the continuation of Bank loan disbursements to Turkey in 1975–79, a period of deteriorating policies: see Anne O. Krueger, "The Role of the World Bank as an International Institution" (Paper presented at a 1982 conference, Mimeographed), 41.

13. For example, the Bank finances only 2.5 percent of capital expenditures if it accounts for as much as 25 percent of total external capital, which in turn finances 10 percent of a country's investment. The point is made by several authors; see, e.g., Krueger, "The Role of the World Bank."

14. Cf. Stanley Please, *The Hobbled Giant*, 36.

15. See "Tenth Annual Review of Project Performance Audit Results, 1984" (World Bank, 1985).

Chapter 7.
Working with Other Sources of Finance

1. Establishment of a secondary market for bank loans is discussed in Jack M. Guttentag and Richard Herring, "Commercial Bank Lending to Less Developed Countries: From Overlending to Underlending to Structural Reform" (World Bank Seminar on Debt and the Developing Countries, Washington, 1984). Ways of insuring bank portfolios are discussed in Henry C. Wallich, *Insurance of Bank Lending to Developing Countries* (New York: Group of Thirty, 1984). The terms of lending can be adapted to the export earnings fluctuations of the borrower in various ways; several possibilities are discussed in Donald Lessard, "North-South: The Implications for Multinational Banking," *Journal of Banking and Finance* (1983). The possible contributions of new and more suitable financial instruments are discussed in Lessard and Williamson, *Financial Intermediation*.

2. See Margaret Garritsen de Vries, *The International Monetary Fund 1972-78*, vol. 2 (Washington: IMF, 1985), 972-974; see also *The Development Committee: Its First Ten Years* (Washington: World Bank, 1984).

3. The Bank's experience with the Caribbean group is reviewed in Robert Kanchuger, "The Caribbean Group," *Finance and Development* 21, 3 (1984).

4. See the 1982 Annual Report of the Chairman of the DAC (Paris: OECD, 1982).

5. Colombia first informally asked the World Bank for assistance in mobilizing external support in 1960, shortly after it had completed its first four-year public investment program. The Bank's response was at first negative since, at the time, it confined its coordination mainly to concessional aid. However, in 1963 the Bank went ahead, in part because Colombia was adopting a consistent set of macroeconomic policies in support of its development plan. The first consultative group meeting, in 1963, was strongly supported by the U.S. government, which wanted to see an increase of such coordination as part of the efforts inspired by the Alliance for Progress. It was attended by the managing director of the IMF, which had worked closely with the Bank in preparatory policy discussions with the Colombian government.

6. See, e.g., the description of a "confrontation" between Colombia and the IMF concerning an exchange rate devaluation in 1966, in Lauchlin Currie, *The Role of Economic Advisers in Developing Countries* (Westport, Conn.: Greenwood Press, 1981), 96-102. The negotiations between Colombia and external agencies in 1966–67 are described in Hayter, *Aid as Imperialism*, 107-119. Colombia's protectionist policies in textiles are described in David Morawetz, *Why the Emperor's New Clothes Are Not Made in Colombia: A Case Study in Latin American and East Asian Manufactured Exports* (New York: Oxford University Press, 1981).

7. See "The Role and Function of the International Monetary Fund" (Washington: IMF, 1985). For long-term use of Fund resources, see Richard Goode, *Economic Assistance to the Developing Countries through the IMF* (Washington: Brookings Institution, 1985), 20, table 2.

8. See Margaret Garritsen de Vries, *The IMF in a Changing World, 1944–85* (Washington: IMF, 1986), 182-198; and *Balance of Payments Adjustment, 1945–86: The IMF Experience* (Washington: IMF, 1987), chaps. 10-12.

9. For example, in Mexico the commercial banks agreed, in March 1985, to consolidate public-sector debt due in 1985–90 and to accept repayment over fourteen years. Similar multiyear agreements

are to be or have been concluded for Brazil, Ecuador, Venezuela, and Yugoslavia. See World Bank, *World Development Report 1985*, 27-29.

10. The Fund obtained a 50 percent increase in quotas, to a total just below SDR 90 billion. In addition, the General Agreement to Borrow was increased from SDR 6.4 billion to 17 billion, and was opened for use by any Fund member whose balance-of-payments problems posed a threat to the stability of the international monetary system. See Margaret Garritsen de Vries, *The IMF in a Changing World*, 191-192.

11. The funds, which are derived from repayments of the credits under the 1976 IMF Trust Fund, must be repaid over ten years (with five-year grace on amortization) and at 0.5 percent interest. Eligible countries include several in sub-Saharan Africa, Bangladesh, Sri Lanka, Bolivia, and Haiti (*IMF Survey*, 31 March 1986).

12. See Mason and Asher, *The World Bank Since Bretton Woods*, chap. 16, esp. 551; and Margaret Garritsen de Vries, *The International Monetary Fund, 1966–71*, vol. 1 (Washington: IMF, 1976), 611, and *The International Monetary Fund, 1972–78*, vol. 2 (Washington: IMF, 1985), 955.

13. See IMF, *World Economic Outlook, April 1985*, table 43.

14. Data from the 1982 Report of the Chairman of the DAC, tables III-1 and III-22 (Paris: OECD, 1982). "Net credits" is gross lending minus loan repayments; "long-term" means a repayment period of over one year.

15. Bond lending also increased significantly in 1970–80, rising in 1981 dollars from $0.8 billion in 1970 to a peak of $7.7 billion in 1978 (see DAC, 1982).

16. See, e.g., Irving S. Friedman, "The Emerging Role of Private Lenders in the Developing World" (New York: Citicorp, 1977), 75-80.

17. For example, the Bank experienced difficulties in implementing "sector conditions" attached to its loans for steel and other heavy industrial facilities in Brazil in the mid-seventies. While these loans served to finance new plants with a clear economic justification, they were made on condition that rational plans be prepared for the expansion of the entire industry in which the plants were located.. The purpose of these conditions was to avoid new investment in heavy industry, which could not be justified by foreseeable demand—an objective often frustrated by easy availability of new credit from other sources, including export credit agencies and private banks.

18. See fn. 9, chap. 5.

19. *World Economic Outlook, April 1986* (Washington: IMF, 1986), table A-42.

20. Estimates from *World Debt Tables, 1986/87*, abridged version (Washington: World Bank, 1987). According to the IMF *World Economic Outlook* (1985), a total of $31 billion of short-term debt was eliminated through restructuring in 1983 and 1984. This trend continued in 1985. Amortization payments to private banks were reduced by $17.5 billion in 1983 and $23 billion in 1984 *below* the levels that would have prevailed in the absence of rescheduling. Further reductions in amortization payments took place in 1985 and 1986.

21. In addition, banks may be encouraged by the institution of a facility to insure part of their portfolio and by an ability to sell loans in a secondary market: see fn. 1. Additional examples are given in *World Development Report 1985* , 121. New lending techniques are also discussed in C. Fred Bergsten, William R. Cline, and John Williamson, *Bank Lending to Developing Countries: The Policy Alternatives* (Washington: Institute for International Economics, 1985), 60-66.

22. This point is also made by Andrew M. Kamarck, "The World Bank and Development: A Personal Perspective," *Finance and Development* 21, 4 (1984).

23. For example, the Bank's financing of the late maturities may be contingent on certain events—e.g., when the market interest rate rises above an agreed level.

24. In total, market placements for B-loan syndications exceeded $1 billion, a relatively significant amount when compared with total new private lending of $7 billion in 1985. More than 90 banks participated in B-loan cofinancing; borrowers were Brazil, Colombia, Hungary, Paraguay, Thailand, and Yugoslavia. Projects were in different sectors, e.g., energy, telecommunications, transportation, and agriculture. The Bank's share was $130 million, a leverage factor of 7:1. Each of the three options was used, including a World Bank guarantee. See T. Ohuchi, "The World Bank and Co-financing" (Statement at a conference in Dubrovnik, Yugoslavia, March 1985); see also George J. Clark, "Proposals to Strengthen World Bank Cofinancing Programs," statement to U.S. House of Representatives, Committee on Banking, Finance and Urban Affairs, Subcommittee on International Development Institutions and Finance, 9 July 1985.

25. See, e.g., *Foreign Direct Investment 1973–87* (New York: Group of Thirty, 1984).

26. See Guisinger, *Investment Incentives*.

27. The 773 projects in 84 countries that the IFC financed through June 1984 represent a total investment of almost $27 billion; the IFC has complemented its own investments of $3.7 billion by $2.5

billion that has been syndicated to other lenders. The IFC has also helped to attract to these projects direct private foreign investment amounting to roughly $1 billion. See *World Development Report 1985*, 132.

28. Data from the *World Development Report 1985*, chap. 9, "Direct and Portfolio Investments."

29. Security markets must meet minimum criteria of liquidity, official regulation, and investment information. The Fund is expected initially to invest in India, Korea, Malaysia, the Philippines, Thailand, Argentina, Brazil, Chile, and Mexico. Other countries under consideration include Jordan, Nepal, and Turkey.

30. See Morgan Guaranty Trust Co., *World Financial Markets* (New York: September 1986).

31. It is estimated that less than 20 percent of net investment flows from DAC member countries to developing countries was guaranteed under national programs in 1977–81. According to OECD sources, only an estimated 9 percent of the existing stock of investment was covered by national schemes at the end of 1981. See Ibrahim Shihata, "Increasing Private Capital Flows to LDCs: The Bank's Proposed Multilateral Investment Guarantee Agency," *Finance and Development* 21, 4 (1984).

32. From "Direct and Portfolio Investments: Their Role in Economic Development," a background paper prepared by World Bank staff for consideration at the Development Committee meeting, 18-19 April 1985.

Chapter 8.
Financing a Growing World Bank

1. The per capita income beyond which the "graduation" policy applies is reviewed each year by the IBRD executive directors.

2. The capital of the IBRD was originally fixed in terms of 1944 U.S. dollars, with each share amounting to $100,000. Since official par values were abandoned under the second amendment of the IMF Articles of Agreement, valuation of IBRD capital in terms of current dollars has been under discussion. For practical purposes, a share has been valued at $120,635 or SDR 100,000, whichever is less. In June 1985 and 1986, a share was calculated at SDR 100,000 ($99,800 in 1985 and $117,800 in 1986).

3. The authorized capital includes a selective increase in capital of $8.4 billion, which was agreed to in May 1984. This increase served to facilitate a realignment in voting shares parallel to changes in

the IMF that occurred in connection with the increase in Fund quotas agreed to in 1983.

4. See Eugene R. Rotberg, *The World Bank: A Financial Appraisal* (Washington: World Bank, 1984), 20.

5. That is, the member countries of the IBRD, which are also members of the DAC of the OECD. On 31 December 1985, the usable portion was 64 percent of IBRD callable capital.

6. Cf. Rotberg, *The World Bank*, 23.

7. *The Washington Post*, 12 April 1986.

8. In 1975–84, the real growth rate of IBRD lending was 5.9 percent per annum; in 1980–84, it slowed to 4.6 percent (Bank lending in current U.S. dollars, deflated by the U.S. price index for capital goods).

9. In this projection the usable portion of the Bank's capital is compared with its net debt—i.e., the Bank's outstanding medium-term obligations minus its liquidity fund. The net debt measures the Bank's impact on capital and money markets; the net debt concept is used by U.S. rating agencies in assessing the security of Bank bonds.

10. See Clausen's speech to the 1985 Annual Meeting of IBRD-IMF Governors.

11. The cofinancing referred to was worked out in 1984 for a Paraguayan livestock development project, for which the Bank lent $25 million. The $15 million cofinancing commercial loan, syndicated by a French bank, has a ten-year maturity with an even service payments flow. Under the agreement, in case the market interest rate exceeds 12 percent (but remains below 16 percent), the additional interest obligation is capitalized into later maturities. The Bank has guaranteed such later maturities and has a contingent liability to finance them. The Bank also used its guarantee for part of the financing package for the Carajas project in Brazil (May 1984).

12. For example, in the case of a loan with a total maturity of twelve years, the Bank guarantee may cover the maturities of the last three years and hence would extend to only one-fourth of the face amount of the loan. If, in addition, the probability of the guarantee being called on is less than one-fifth, the likely claim against the Bank's capital need not exceed one-twentieth of the loan amount. Hence, the Bank would effectively achieve a gearing ratio of 1:5 if its guarantees the entire loan and 1:20 if it guarantees only the maturities in the last three years.

13. From discussion with Nicholas Hope of the World Bank staff.

14. See Phaup, *The World Bank*.

15. Percentages are for IDA commitments relative to official development assistance (ODA) in 1981.

16. See *IDA in Retrospect* (New York: Oxford University Press, 1982), 5.

17. Inflation measured by the U.S. wholesale price index for capital goods (*International Financial Statistics*, IMF).

18. *IDA in Retrospect*; *IDA-7 Replenishment* (Washington: Overseas Development Council (ODC), 1984); and the 1985 *World Bank Annual Report*, 22.

19. See *Toward Sustained Development in Sub-Saharan Africa*.

20. See *IDA in Retrospect*: "The Industrial Import Programs did not become a vehicle for reforms in specific industries, despite attempts to improve the dialogue on industrial policy. But they did help support some broader policy shifts" (56).

21. Ibid., 55.

22. *IDA in Retrospect* lists 28 countries that are former IDA recipients (24).

23. *IDA in Retrospect*, 28.

24. From January 1982 to January 1985 the IBRD also charged a front-end fee payable when the loan became effective. For FY 1984 the fee was lowered in two steps from 1.5 percent to 0.25 percent. In view of the IBRD earnings performance, the fee has not been levied since January 1985.

Chapter 9.
The Politics of the World Bank

1. Bauer, *Equality, the Third World and Economic Delusion*, 132; see also Phaup, *The World Bank*, 30-33.

2. See "The U.S. Participation in the Multilateral Development Banks in the 1980s," U.S. Department of the Treasury, 1982.

3. Phaup, *The World Bank*, 52.

4. Ibid., 46-47.

5. Ibid., 52.

6. See *Aid for Development: The Key Issues* (Washington: World Bank, 1986), chap. 3, "Support for Aid."

7. See the conference report (Washington: ODC, 1986).

8. See Masoni, "Non-Governmental Organizations and Development."

Chapter 10.
Facing the Future

1. See, e.g., Harold Lever and Christopher Huhne, *Debt and Danger: The World Financial Crisis* (Harmondsworth, Middlesex, England: Penguin Books, 1985).

2. See Avramovic and Assoc., *Economic Growth and External Debt*, esp. J.P. Hayes, "Long-Run Growth and Debt Servicing Problems, Projections of Debt Servicing Burdens and the Conditions of Debt Failure"; see also Barend A. de Vries, "The Debt-Bearing Capacity of Developing Countries: A Comparative Analysis," *Banca Nazionale del Lavoro Quarterly Review* (March 1971).

3. See, e.g., David Knox, "Resuming Growth in Latin America," *Finance and Development* 22, 3 (1985).

Index

A

Africa (sub-Saharan)
  capital flows to, 42–43
  performance of, 41–44
  private sector in, 49
  Special Facility for, 43, 127, 141, 157
  World Bank reports on, 41n
Agricultural research, 21
Agriculture, 20–24
Aid
  bilateral: relations with World Bank, 5
  coordination of, 82–87, 153
  critics of, 1–5
  effectiveness of, 4
Alliance for Progress, 136
Alter, Gerald M., 58n
Asher, Robert E., *See* Mason, Edward S.
Avramovic, D., 13n, 149n
Ayers, Robert L., 7n

B

Baker, James A., III, 48, 86, 96
Balassa, Bela, 30n

Baldwin, George B., 64n
Bangladesh, 128
Bauer P.T., 3–4, 136
Baum, Warren C. 21n
Bergsten, C. Fred, 97n
Bernstein, Edward M., 91
Black, Eugene R., 11, 62
Brandt Commission, 3
Brazil
  economic performance of, 47–48
  lending to, 97
  World Bank assessment of, 74
Bretton Woods
  Conference, 8
    presence of developing countries, 8n
  Committee, 143

C

Capital
  flight, 47
  flows to developing countries, 34–35
Chenery, Hollis B., 18
China

177

J

K

About the Author

Educated at the universities of Utrecht and Chicago and the Massachusetts Institute of Technology, Dr. Barend A. de Vries has worked in the International Monetary Fund and the World Bank, has taught economics at a number of universities, and has published many articles and papers on international economic and development issues. In the IMF he participated in missions to both industrial and developing countries, and undertook analyses of the trade and price effects of exchange rate changes. In the World Bank, in both economic and operating positions, including those of chief economist and director of creditworthiness studies, he helped develop and direct research and worked on problems of country strategies, external debt, export policies, and industrial competitiveness. Throughout his career he has collaborated with officials in Latin America and other developing countries in the planning and implementation of their economic policies.